Journey with the students of Palisades Christian Academy and Upper Columbia Academy as they share words, chosen through prayer, to bring us closer to God. As part of our Active and Authentic Learning emphasis, these ideas were inspired in Pastor Sid Hardy, Pastor Fred Riffel, and Pastor Kevin Wilfley's Bible classes. The rhetoric was refined in Geoff Heald, Karyl Kramer, Stephen Lacey, Ruth Lenz, Michelle Melendy, and Rachel Riffel's English classes. Shelley Bacon graciously edited the book. The cover is digital artwork and was designed by Carly Haeger. Bob Lenz along with the student editors Carly Haeger and Ashley Olson designed and formatted the pages and text. Our title, *Chosen*, is the Associated Student Body's theme for this year.

We pray these devotional thoughts will inspire the next step on God's chosen path for you.

Letters from our Principals

Welcome to our third annual student devotional designed and written by students. I pray this devotional will not only draw you closer to Christ but will also give you a glimpse into the hearts of our amazing students. I appreciate very much the theme selected for this devotional. Each one of us are chosen and called by God to be His sons and daughters. UCA is thrilled to be able to partner with Palisades Christian Academy again this year to produce this book. I pray you are blessed as you read these stories from our UCA and PCA students.

Blessings,
Eric Johnson
Principal, Upper Columbia Academy

This year's theme is "chosen". "Chosen" can mean something is being selected, if used as a verb. It is wise to stop and ponder the importance of the selection process and choices we make, with an eye the to the potential outcomes. "Chosen" can also be used as an adjective, to describe something as special, such as Jesus was the "Chosen One." This devotional was written from the hearts of our students. They wanted to share something meaningful, which we pray will help you through life's complicated journey. As you read, may you be reminded that our choices have eternal potential, and no matter what comes, you will always be special to Him.

Monte Fisher
Principal, Palisades Christian Academy

The Chosen King
~ Isaac Acker ~

The theme for our school year is "Chosen," and one of the most chosen people in the Bible is David. He was chosen directly by God, speaking through his prophet Samuel. He was chosen over all his older siblings who seemed, on the outside, to be clearly better leaders and probably better looking. That God would pick him specifically for leading His people shows how good his heart really was. Not only was he chosen, but he was also a man God said was a man after His own heart. We can look at the story of David and learn a lot of stuff from his life.

David's story teaches us that it does not matter in the long run what we look like on the outside and that God only looks on what is in our hearts. God will choose you no matter what other people think of you. No matter how mean people may be to you there is always a light at the end of the tunnel. God values you a lot more than anyone on Earth ever can. If God can take a lowly farmer and turn him into a king, what can He do for you? God will see what your heart really looks like, and He will judge you on that not your outward appearance.

Trusting in God's Plan
~ Jonah Alvarado ~

Let's face it, everyone has felt worried, stressed, and discouraged about the future, but these worries take a big toll on our health and relationships. We often forget they have solutions: all we must do is trust in God.

I have been homeschooled all my life, and in my family, it's a tradition to go to boarding school for high school. My family was already making plans for sending my brother and me away, and I was not happy about it. I had many friends and was living comfortably at home. Why did I have to leave home and go to some foreign school away from my friends and family? My parents asked me to pray and not to think so harshly about it.

Six months went by and summer was starting to come to an end. My parents were still unsure of where to send my brother and me, and they prayed very hard about what they should do. One day out of the blue, an old friend texted me. After catching up, she asked me if I was going to her school. Surprised, I asked if the school was going to be open. She said it was, so I promised I would talk to my parents about it. Four days later, I transferred to Upper Columbia Academy.

My testimony isn't much, but it just shows that even though your life may look set and complete, God always has a plan for what is going to happen. You may not be happy about it, but remember to trust in God and know that He is doing it in your best interest. *"Trust in the Lord with all your heart, and do not lean on your understanding"* (Proverbs 3:5).

God's Love
~ Micah Alvarado ~

Do you love dogs? Well, so do I. Don't you just love it when dogs are so loving, caring, obedient and protective?

There's a story called, "Jamie, Where Are You?" It talks about a family who has a deaf son named Jaime, and a dog named Chief. One weekend, Jamie's family was all busy around the house. His father was mowing the lawn, his mother was doing the dishes, and his grandma was sweeping the garage. Jamie was in the backyard deck playing with Chief. As grandma was sweeping, she could hear Chief barking constantly. She finally went over to the backyard and noticed Jamie was missing. Soon everyone panicked and desperately looked for Jamie. Quickly, the family realized that Jamie was in the cooler. Jami was minutes from death. If Chief had not kept barking at the cooler, Jami most likely wouldn't have been found in time.

The love of a dog towards its master is like God's love to us. Jesus died on the cross to save us from sin. Jesus gave His life for us to be saved.

"And the Lord shall deliver me from every evil work, and will preserve me unto his heavenly kingdom: to whom be glory for ever and ever. Amen" (2 Timothy 4:18).

Respect Yourself
~ Aby Avendano ~

"For God did not give us a spirit of timidity, but a spirit of power, of love and of self-discipline" (2 Timothy 1:7).

Give to yourself enthusiastically.
Treat yourself with generosity.
Forgive yourself harmoniously.
Trust yourself confidently and completely.
You know what is right and best for you.
Listen to your own small inner voice; do not ignore its urgings.
Above all, love yourself wholeheartedly.
Just remember, you are working to improve yourself.
And what person in your life is worth working to improve you.
Take good care of yourself.
You are important to the entire world.
More importantly… you are important to YOU!

Self-respect is a valuable trait that will cause you to become the greatest version of yourself. When you value yourself; you in turn are well-fashioned to influence others and add worth to their lives. A healthy body, mind, soul, and spirit has the power to carry you to greater heights and challenges in times to come. When you properly take care of your wellbeing, you will be more encouraged to fulfill the things God has waiting for you to achieve. When you are upset or in need of assistance, ask God to give you the wisdom to know how to live a well-balanced life that brings honor, glory, and praise to His name.

Chosen by UCA
~ Christian Barela ~

To be honest I am not sure why I came here, but my family said I got accepted for a reason. I am hoping that reason is good because I left all my friends and family back home.

I have learned new things here at UCA: a lot about science and God. They teach differently here from what I have seen. Everyone here surprised me in so many ways. I have seen people wanting to help others, which I am not used to at all.

Being here you need to change in a good way, so I'm trying to change and be nicer. I am trying to be a better person in general.

Maybe God gave me a second chance to change. Maybe He wants me to change so He can use me for His work, and I am willing to do His work.

I was one of the chosen. God wanted me to see that, and now I do.

Don't Forget that He is King
~ Ethan Barker ~

"Let us consider how we may spur one another on toward love and good deeds . . . encouraging one another—and all the more as you see the Day approaching" (Hebrews 10:24-25).

In the U.S. and other parts of the world today, we are living in an anti-Cristian culture. More and more people are rejecting Christianity and the church and saying they have no religion. It is heartbreaking to see people leave God's church, and the pressures to change to a faithless culture seem to be increasing all the time.

As I was going through Hebrews recently, it gave me a new perspective. As we hear about Jesus, what He has done for us, and about Him being King over everything, we should naturally be encouraged in our faith in Christ. But the pressures and challenges remain.

Even if we experience despair and discouragement, we are encouraged to hold tight to the one who is faithful. All other things may fail us, but Jesus is faithful. His promises are true. Even when we experience discouragement and despair, He is faithful.

Let us continue to encourage each other, even if we come across difficult areas of our lives. As our message for this year is the word "Chosen," we must remember that we are chosen by God, the One who has the world in His hand and the One who notices when one of the smallest creatures falls. If that is so, why do we question and fail to trust Him in different situations when times get tough? We should not trust in one who is unreliable; we must trust in the One who is faithful. Let us continue to be encouraged and to encourage one another in the Lord.

The End of Time
~ Austin Benado ~

The end of time is not the most encouraging thought. We have all heard the verses of how the earth will fall apart, people will quit their religion, and chaos will occur. I do not know about any of you, but this is a scary thought for me. But when people are all talking about the bad, you should always find the good. The second coming of the Father is soon—very soon. The world as we know it is crumbling. Fires are raging, people are protesting, and COVID-19 has taken over the world. Does this not sound like the end of time? I believe that we aren't that far from the second coming of Jesus Christ. Every minute we are closer to seeing His heavenly face as He rides down through the clouds with His angels next to Him.

If you haven't accepted God as your Savior, I highly encourage you to do it. God doesn't want anything more than for you to accept and know that His love is never failing. Satan is working double time trying to get people to his side and not to accept God. We need to keep our faith more than ever now. Satan is not backing down; he knows that he's not going to win against God, so he's trying his very hardest to get as many people as he can to his side.

Recently a family friend was corrupted by a demon. This man is so God-like he would never miss an opportunity to help others. The point is that Satan is working really hard right now, and he won't back down unless you accept God as your Father, Friend, and Creator. Things will get rough, but we have to hold on to what we believe and never let down our faith.

Arrogant for Help
~ Isai Blanco ~

Arrogance is a very bad habit of mine. I am so prideful and self-centered that I don't ask for help—not even from my parents. I don't ask because I believe asking for help makes me look like a hopeless child. Now I regret this and realize that if I had just asked for help, I would have been more successful in my school life.

I could have let go of my arrogance earlier and had a more fruitful life. I was too confident and unaware of the whole list of people who would have helped me. But, again, I thought asking for help meant I had no place in higher classes.

Eventually, I went to a meeting with Dean Hess and Mr. Hartman. I was so far behind that I could not hope to finish all the work on my own. They asked me if I wanted help, and I realized that if I could just say "yes," everything would be better . . . so I did. And that one small word let me do things I could not do on my own.

God, too, is waiting for us to say "yes."

God First
~ Logan Bodnar ~

One of the difficulties I have had in my life is learning that God is the one I need to ask for help. In the past, I have always relied entirely on help from others and not even stopped to think what God's plan was. I tend to like to stick to others' ideas because it is an easy way for me to feel like I have everything figured out and organized, but, in reality, all I am doing is letting someone else control who I am. I am not saying that taking others' advice is a bad thing, and it can be a great way to identify your problems and resolve them, but usually it is a good idea to stop and take a moment to ask God what He wants us to be doing.

In hard times, it is always a good idea to get help from others you trust, but take some time to make sure you are doing what God wants you to do. God has chosen us to be part of His plan, and we need to make sure we are doing our part. *"So be careful to do what the Lord your God has commanded you; do not turn aside to your right, or to your left"* (Deuteronomy 5:32).

Crafts & Christ
~ Gianna Bolla ~

Me? Chosen to teach arts and crafts to these messy kids with their sticky hands and intolerance to obedience? No way! I was not fond of the idea of leading out craft time for a group of preschoolers. I mean, could they even comprehend the correct way to use scissors?

Realizing my impatience and lack of ability to handle children, I was apprehensive when my church leaders asked if I would be interested in working at Vacation Bible School. My hesitance in deciding if I would participate was clear; nevertheless, I said yes. When the designated Monday morning finally came, I headed off, anxious about how the day's events would turn out. Throughout the week I was definitely busy. I taught the kids various crafts like how to make paper buildings, draw pictures, and build small toys.

At the end of the week, with their goofy grins and tight hugs around my legs, I had grown a soft spot for all the kids I had met. I learned patience and improved my leadership abilities. I may not have known beforehand, but I truly feel God had a reason for calling me there. Because of my experience that first summer, I have gone back every year, and the feeling of warmth and joy never fades.

Throughout our lives we may feel God calling us to something out of our comfort zones. It's been something that's hard for me, but I've learned to trust in Him because He has a plan in our lives, and works through us in many ways. Sometimes it's those new and challenging experiences that bring us closer to Him. Always remember *"The Lord your God has chosen you out of all the nations on the earth, to be His own"* (Deuteronomy 7:6).

The Prize
~ Tya Bourget ~

"I press on toward the goal to win the prize for which God has called me heavenward in Christ Jesus" (Philippians 3:14).

It was just me and her. Hearts pounding. Heads sweating. Heavily breathing. In that moment it was just me and her. I was determined to go on no matter how tired I was. I was going to win that trophy.

"HAJIME!" the sensei yelled.

We started. Both missing a throw or trip. Finally, I managed to flip the other girl. I started to pin her, using all my might to keep her down. I was getting weaker and weaker, but too determined to win that trophy to stop.

"Iipon sore made," the sensei called, declaring the end of the match. He declared the winner and then we bowed to each other. I shook my opponent's hand as a sign of respect, then walked off the mat.

Like my story, we should all keep going even when it gets hard. We should follow God and do the tasks that He has made for us to do. He has sent us to the world to do everything through Him, to show the world that there is a prize in Heaven waiting for us.

God's Chosen
~ Lyndi Brenton ~

The room was still and hushed in awe as a lovely young maiden entered the room. Every eye was fastened on her as she slowly made her way forward to where the king of Persia sat. He too seemed to be enraptured by her beauty. He smiled as he said in a decisive tone, "Yes, you shall be my queen." Esther was not a girl from high society. To all outsiders, she seemed like any other Jewish girl. She faced trials as well as joys just like everyone else. Her parents had died when she was young, and she had been raised by her God-fearing Uncle Mordecai. Although she was just an ordinary girl, the story of Queen Esther is well known. Her bravery to stand for her people, even risking her own life for those she loved, has been admired by many.

Each one of us is an Esther. Each one of us has the potential to do something great. It may not be becoming queen of Persia and saving the Jewish nation. However, it might be eating lunch with the new kid at school or visiting an elderly neighbor. We have all been called by God. He has chosen us for a special purpose and no one is insignificant in His eyes.

"Therefore, as God's chosen people, holy and dearly loved, clothe yourselves with compassion, kindness, humility, gentleness and patience. Bear with each other and forgive one another if any of you has a grievance against someone. Forgive as the Lord forgave you. And over all these virtues put on love, which binds them all together in perfect unity" (Colossians 3:12-14).

Chosen Like a Rose
~ Felicity Broome ~

If you didn't know, roses represent love and passion from the Greek god Eros. They are mostly bought for Valentine's Day since it is a holiday about love and passion. When you buy them, you always look for the best ones, the "flawless" ones. No one really goes for the less bloomed or the wilting ones. They go for the typical, simple, and boring rose. The ones that are "pleasing" to the eye or "elegant."

But to God, all roses are unique, eye catching, and outstanding, even if we think they are "too small" or "too big," God thinks they are all perfect. Did you know God also has a Heavenly rose garden? The roses represent us, His children, and the fruit represents our growth in Him. Each one of us is different from one other. He loves all the colors of the roses no matter how bright or colorful they are, but black has a different meaning than the rest. Even though black means a new start in life, black roses are known to represent mourning and death, which Satan represents if we follow him. The white roses represent purity and we become pure when we go to heaven, if we choose Him. God wants us, His little children, in heaven planted in His garden. The question is, do you want to be chosen or picked?

"But the rich should take pride in their humiliation—since they will pass away like a wildflower. For the sun rises with scorching heat and withers the plant; its blossom fall and its beauty will be destroyed. In the same way, the rich will fade away even while they go about their business" (James 1:10, 11).

Finding Value
~ Katie Bunn ~

"Before I formed you in the womb I knew you, and before you were born I consecrated you; I appointed you a prophet to the nations" (Jeremiah 1:5).

Sometimes it is hard to believe that we are all important to God. We look at other people's achievements and traits and feel we could not ever be as good as they are at doing God's will. I personally have felt this way before, feeling as though many other people could do everything better than I. A good example of this was in fifth grade. I was at a new school, with new people, having just moved into a new house that year also. I felt, as most new kids do, that I would never fit in or find new friends in this strange and unfamiliar territory.

During those first few weeks, I compared myself to other people and thought of how this person had a better project, or how someone knew so much more history than I did, or how much smarter everyone seemed. As the weeks turned into months, however, I started to find some great friends, and see my own work as valuable too. During math class, I found I had a different way of looking at a problem, and it was not wrong; it was just not the same as the next person. I started to see how my way of thinking was unique, just as important.

This is how God sees us all—different, but all valuable. Even though everyone might seem better than us or more important, God loves us all the same, no one above any other. We are here to do His work at different times, in our own way. God calls us all and will help us no matter where we are.

He Will Teach You
~ Angie Buursma ~

Imagine this, as you walk into the temple in Jerusalem, you watch the ceremony of the sacrificial lamb. And as you watch, you realize the lamb represents you. How would you feel? I don't know about you, but that would just scare me half to death. To think at the age of 12, Jesus, during the Passover feast, watched the ceremony of the sacrificial lamb and realized what it really meant: That He would one day be that sacrifice. That must have been such a burden especially for a 12-year-old boy. Can you just picture Jesus dallying behind, pondering all that He had seen? I believe God was teaching His Son, preparing Him for the journey that lay ahead.

God loves you very much, and He wants to teach you and prepare you for what lies ahead in your spiritual journey, just as He taught and prepared His son, Jesus. All you have to do is make the choice to spend time with Him every day, and He will do the rest. He will change you into His image. He has chosen you for something very special. Will you now choose Him and let Him into your heart? The journey won't always be easy, but in the end, you will never regret the choice you made no matter what happens to you in this sinful world.

Jeremiah 10:1-2 says, *"Hear ye the word which the Lord speaketh unto to you, O house of Israel: Thus saith the Lord, Learn not the way of the heathen, and be not dismayed at the signs of heaven; for the heathen are dismayed at them."*

Greater Love has No One
~ Caterina Carlson ~

I look to my left and right to find two beautiful young ladies who have been there for me through thick and thin. I find the three of us sitting on our two twin sized beds pushed together to make one big bed with a single strand of lights plugged in above our heads. At this point we have just enough light to see our textbooks and do our homework that is due the next day. I sit here at 11:45 PM on a Thursday night looking around me and I see God working in my life. Even though we have a two-thirds chance of getting caught and getting at least 30 minutes of community service, we are staying up all night to help each other get homework done.

I believe God puts certain people in our lives right here next to us for a reason. These are the nights I will remember for my high school years, the moments the three of us freeze up because we hear a creek in the floor outside our door, the moments of us sharing secrets or cutting our hair. The late-night tears as we take a cold long walk through our past again, or just flat out die laughing over a crack in the wall.

In every moment like this you experience, God chooses to have those certain people share the moments with you. So, my advice to everyone is when you get into fights with your closest friends, remember that God wanted you to cry and laugh with them. One of my favorite quotes from the Bible shows just how much friends really do matter:

"Greater love has no one than this, that someone lay down his life for his friends" (John 15:13).

Average
~ Claire Christensen ~

Have you ever felt average? Maybe you feel like you are not amazing at a sport, but not super bad either. Or you do not get the best grades, but you are still passing. Sometimes maybe you feel like you are too average and boring for God to use you or see you. I know I have felt like that before, but I know for a fact it is not true!

Take David for example. Before God revealed his plans, David was your average kid. He was the youngest, but he was by no means the baby of the family. If anything, he was the forgotten child. He probably was not even that good looking or tall at that point in his life like his brothers are said to have been. He was just the kid with the harp that watched the sheep. When the prophet Samuel came to his house to find the next king of Israel, his parents and siblings did not even think to get him. He was just out caring for the sheep, forgotten by everyone else. However, even though the rest of the world thought his smarter, more impressive-looking brothers would make better kings, God still chose David.

To me, this story really demonstrates that even if you do not feel important or talented, God can still use you to do amazing things if you only trust in Him. Next time you feel ignored or like just an average person floating through life with no purpose, remember God created you to do amazing things. *"Can a woman forget her nursing child, that she should have no compassion on the son of her womb? Even these may forget, yet I will not forget you"* (Isaiah 49:15).

Adopted
~ Elise Colburn ~

My dog, Chewbacca (Chewie), is friendly and energetic. He loves attention and will sit, pleading with his eyes, until the target pets him. We don't even have to take him to "go" anymore—he runs out through the dog door and does his business on his own! But my sweet terrier wasn't always this comfortable.

He was just one year old when we adopted him. He trembled when a person touched him, and his ears were tucked tightly back in fright. For months, he wouldn't let my little brother pet him. He was scared of us and other people, and he didn't feel comfortable in our house.

But slowly, his behavior began to change. He learned to trust us and to feel safe in our house. We became Chewie's people, and the house his home. It took longer for him to be comfortable around visitors, but finally he managed it. Our little border terrier is happy with us, and I can't imagine life without him.

God changes us in much the same way. We are adopted, sin and all. He brings love and peace into our lives, and through His Spirit, we become more like Him.

"And I am sure of this, that He who began a good work in you will bring it to completion at the day of Jesus Christ" (Philippians 1:6).

Go to the Dog, You Worry Wart
~ Bex Colcord ~

I do not know about you, but I worry entirely too much. What should I wear? What do they think of me? What am I going to do with my life? What even is the meaning of life? Why does it matter? Dogs do not worry about stuff like that. They live, love, and enjoy playing fetch. We could all learn a little from them. I believe that God left little reminders of His love and how we can fully embrace that all over the world. Dogs are one of those reminders. So today, relax, do not stress about tomorrow, hang out with your favorite person and just enjoy all the little pleasures that life has to offer. Forget about your issues, problems and all your frustrations. Just let life take you where you need to go. Most importantly, have fun.

"Therefore, I tell you, do not worry about your life, what you will, eat or drink; or about your body, what you will wear. Is not life more than food, and the body more than clothes?" (Matthew 6:25).

"Cast all your anxiety on Him because He cares about you" (1 Peter 5:7).

Dirt Bike Accident
~ Jeremy Colvin ~

One day my friend and I decided to go dirt biking with his Dad. The thing is, their bikes were faster than mine, so when we got to the trail, they just took off and left me behind. When I caught up to them, they were waiting for me. But when it was time to go back to the truck, they just booked it and left me behind again. This time, I was lost and didn't know which way to go. I tried to go the right way, but all the sudden I crashed my bike into a stump and could not start it. All I could not do was wait for them to find me.

I waited for a long time. It was getting dark, and I started to panic! I was scared because I was a long way from the truck. When I finally heard a dirt bike, I yelled at the top of my lungs so they could hear me and rescue me. When my friend's dad found me, I was so excited and scared at the same time. I was excited because I knew someone was close but still scared he might not find me. When he found me, he was able to turn on the reserve gas and started my bike.

"Don't worry about anything; instead, pray about everything. Tell God what you need and thank Him for all He has done" (Philippians 4:6).

INSPIRATION
~ Daniel Cook ~

I used to be full of inspiration; words and rhythms would come to me like food to my mouth. Inspiration does not come to everyone though; some people have a hard time being creative and must look at other people's ideas and thoughts to think of something on their own. Because I have always been full of creativity, ideas, and INSPIRATION, I have always been able to think of creative things fast.

I remember a time not long ago when I was going through a rough patch, I could not think of anything. It was like my talent abandoned me. During this time I was very unhappy and full of self-doubt. It was about three months of constant pain and excruciating moments of silence. Then I went on a trip with a good friend who was a pastor and we connected well. We went to a lake up in the mountains of Washington. As we were up there, he talked a lot about God and His plan. He knew I was going through a rough time and eventually got me to come out and tell him how my life was going. He then asked if he could pray for me, and out of respect I said "Of course." He prayed a strong prayer. After he was done, I felt like a weight I could not carry before was being lifted for me, and something terrible left me. My inspiration then came back; I was able to write music, sing, and smile again.

God spoke through a friend and gave me inspiration again; He helped me find myself when I could not. God is Inspiration, it comes from Him, and if we let Him in, He will fill us with INSPIRATION.

God Gave Us a House
~ Nathan Coon ~

"Therefore I tell you, whatever you ask in prayer, believe that you have received it, and it will be yours" (Mark 11:24).

The summer after I turned nine years old, my family sold our home and were moving to a new town. We couldn't move into our new home for a few weeks to a month. So we stayed in a hotel for a few days and then stayed in the boy's dorm at our local academy until we could move into our new house.

After living in the dorm for almost a week, my parents went to town to sign the papers for the house. They had to turn around and come back to the dorm because they forgot their checkbook. As they were coming back, they got a call about another house that was available and was close to our church and school. They called the landlord, and he said that they could stop by since the key was above the door. When they saw the house, they said they liked it, and the landlord said that we could move in the next day.

All this, from when my parents turned around to get the checkbook, to when they looked at the house and were told we could move in, happened in about thirty to forty minutes. It was an answer to prayer because we could move in immediately, and it had a lot of things we wanted: it was in the country, close to our church and school, and it had a wood stove and a well. Like Mark said in the verse above, *"Whatever you ask in prayer… it will be yours."*

Chosen
~ Carson Cox ~

I am sure we have all heard of David, right? A guy who played the harp, killed a giant, and became king. But something you may not know is how old he was. According to numerous Bible scholars, David was only 12-15 years old, standing under 5' tall when he killed the nearly 10' tall giant! That is younger than 75% of our school and he was still able to do something amazing.

So now you are thinking, "Okay, thanks for the useless fact, Carson," but it wasn't just a fact. Many times I find myself wondering if my life has a purpose, and if I am just one out of 113 billion people who have lived on the earth and figured nearly nothing out. I need to remind myself that God CHOSE me to do something big. I may be young, small, unaccomplished, and many other things, but wasn't David?

The Play Book
~ Isaac Dant ~

I am a Green Bay Packers fan. I have always loved football and play it whenever I can. I also think about it a lot and can see where it effects my daily life.

When you train in football, you practice different plays and get familiar with the play book. Although studying the play book is boring and requires a lot of concentration, when you have the play book memorized, you will be able to know exactly what to expect and how to do whatever you need to do, and to do it to the best of your ability. It is very important for both the quarter back and receiver to practice, so that even when things get chaotic, all of the hard work and consideration will pay off, and they both will be able to communicate and execute the play.

It is the same with our relationship with God. The playbook is the Bible and the Ten Commandments. We need to read, get familiar with and study them. Then after we are familiar with the Bible and talk to God through prayer, we can know what God wants. We will be able to communicate during chaotic times, like the Coronavirus messing up our lives and making us stay home. If you keep communication with God, you will know His plan even during the Coronavirus.

Psalms 144:1 says, *"Praise the Lord! He is my Rock. He prepares me for war. He trains me for battle."*

Chosen
~ Micah Dant ~

When I first thought of going to UCA, I was very nervous. I thought I would have a hard time making friends and fitting in. Since I am shy and was coming from a small school, I didn't think I would do well in a bigger school. When school started, I just hung out with the few friends I already had. I thought I would focus on my work and get good grades, but I was very wrong.

When Mr. Hess told me that there was freshman retreat, I was excited and I thought that I would be able to hang out with just the two friends I had in my class, but again I was wrong. When we got onto the bus, they took our phones. There and then I realized this would be a long weekend with a lot of people I thought were weird and people I didn't know. The next day the seniors and staff made us do team building activities involving our whole class. Our class had to flip a tarp while we all stood on it. Our class failed terribly, and we ended up spending four and a half hours on the tarp until the staff told us how to complete the task. Once the weekend was over, I knew everyone, and for the first time that year I felt close to my classmates.

In 1 Thessalonians 1:4 it says, *"For we know, brothers and sisters loved by God, that He has chosen you."* This verse reminds me that even though I didn't think I would be chosen, I will always be chosen by God.

Elisha and the Big Bad Bears
~ Zach Davis ~

We should listen to God or we are going to die! Wait a minute, let me explain. You might not actually die, but your life will be difficult, and you will have to face the consequences of your actions.

In the Bible there is a story of Elisha and the bears. In this story Elisha was going up to a place called Bethel, and as he was walking along, some kids came out of the town and jeered at him saying, *"Go on up you bald head, go on up you bald head.' Elisha then turned around, looked at them and called a curse down on them in the name of the Lord. Then two hungry bears came out of the woods and chased the kids, with drool coming out of their mouths and stomachs, and mauled all forty-two of the youths"* (2 Kings 2:23-24).

The moral of this story is even though you may not get eaten by bears, you should still listen to God, or you will have to face trials and tribulations.

Clarity
~ Lindsay Demitor ~

"I am leaving with you a gift – peace of mind and heart. And the peace I give is a gift the world cannot give. So, don't be troubled or afraid" (John 14:27).

God is always in the back of my mind or on my shoulder telling me what to do and how to tell right from wrong. I cannot really explain my love for God, but He is constantly blessing me, and I am over the moon for Him, ha-ha. He clears out all the negativity whenever I pray about it. It sounds kind of strange, but I like putting all my issues onto God, and I think He enjoys it too! In my opinion we all need a good friend to confide in when we are lost and overwhelmed, and God is mine. He has opened my mind to so many things and helped me get in the habit of treating people with kindness, letting go, forgiving, etc. He has also taught me how to love myself. I am His, and I should be proud of everything He has made of me. John 14:27 perfectly describes what God does for us, and we never need to worry when we have His love.

Sent to UCA
~ Matthew Demitor ~

When I was younger, I attended Rogers Adventist School for kindergarten, and then from first grade to freshman year I went to a College Place public school. But for my sophomore year, since my sister was becoming a freshman, my Dad wanted us to go to UCA together because the public-school system was not the best environment for my sister and me.

At first, my sister and I were not too happy to leave all of our friends, but my Dad and my oldest sister Jessica attended UCA, and they both loved it, so my Dad insisted that we would love it too. And so far, everyone I have met has been very friendly and accepting. All the teachers have been great, and I enjoy going to class each day (mostly). I believe that God has brought my sister and me to UCA for a reason. I have yet to figure that reason out, but I am sure I will in time.

"For I know the plans I have for you, plans to prosper you and not to harm you, plans to give you hope and a future" (Jeremiah 29:11).

Heavenly Mail
~ Hadassa DePaula ~

I was at a youth conference in Idaho, and Sabbath afternoon they always do an outreach activity, but this year would be different because of COVID-19. Instead of knocking on doors and handing out literature, we would be leaving a bag, with a Great Controversy and an invitation to a health seminar, on people's doorstep. This was discouraging because the biggest blessing about outreach is getting to talk to people.

A good friend of mine and I started down the street hanging bags on door handles. After about five minutes she said, "Why don't we pray and ask God to send people out of their homes so we can talk them?" So we paused on the sidewalk and said a quick prayer. Within just a few minutes people started coming out of their houses to check the mail. We got to talk to person after person; it was as though everyone decided to check their mail at the same time.

One lady stands out to me. She came out to check her mail just as we were walking by. We approached her. My friend introduced us and then handed her the bag and explained what was inside. The lady went on to refuse the book and began telling us why she wasn't interested. Silently I prayed that if she needed the book that she would change her mind and take it. Just as we were about to say "alright" and leave, she said "You know what, I'll take the book and read it. It sounds interesting."

God works in miraculous ways. So often we are tempted to think that God doesn't listen to our prayers. But He does listen. That day we handed out over 1,000 Great Controversies. God truly does hear and answer prayers!

Safety in Jesus
~ Hannah DePaula ~

"The angel of the Lord encampeth round about them that fear [love] Him, and delivereth them" (Psalms 34:7).

The sun was already up and promised another hot day in Monapools Game Reserve. It was Sabbath morning for the missionaries in the Savannahs of Zimbabwe, Africa. For the parents, Sabbath School and Church were very important. The kids, however, wanted to explore the bush and begged to go for a walk along the river embankment to a watering hole.

Persistence quickly prevailed, and a group of kids and parents were soon walking toward the watering hole. As the group walked along, conversation turned to the tall grass and trees that provided shade on the one side of the trail. What if there was a pride of lions sleeping in the shade among the grass? Would the group of kids awaken the wild animals who were lurking in the shadows? The group walked on teasing each other and pretending to scare one another. When the group arrived safely back at camp, those who slept through the heat of the day were anxious to leave for the routine evening game drive and decided to drive down the road that paralleled the trail on the other side of the grass to the same water hole that was visited on the walk. Enthusiastically everyone loaded into the van. They had not gone far when one of the kids exclaimed, "Lions!" To everyone's amazement and realization, they had walked past a pride of over twelve lions sleeping in the shade just hours before.

In Psalms 34:7 God promises His protection to all that love Him. And in 1 Peter 5:8 we are warned to *"Be sober, be vigilant; because your adversary the devil, as a roaring lion, walketh about, seeking whom he may devour."*

Preparation Through Faith
~ Duran Downes ~

God prepares you for things you do not know are going to happen in the future. You may face challenges that lead to bigger challenges. He always has a purpose. Take David for example. David was a shepherd who tended to his father's sheep. He had many problems during his life.

At a very young age he was killing bears with his bare hands. He used a sling to defeat other animals who would prey on his herd. Take the lion he killed. He may have killed multiple lions, but just think about one. It was a miracle for Samson, who was of great stature and strength, to kill a lion. David did it as well when he was probably in his teens. It was way crazier of a thing for God to do to help David, a young man, kill a lion.

David's faith was tested all the time and all of these things led to him fighting Goliath, who can't even be compared to a lion.

Knowing all of this, we should never be scared of anything and should always have faith in God. If David did it, you could do it. So always trust that you are preparing for something larger.

Attentive
~ Melani Dubon ~

"For you created my inmost being; you knit me together in my mother's womb. I praise you because I am fearfully and wonderfully made; your works are wonderful; I know that full well" (Psalm 139: 13-14).

When I think of words that describe God, I think of just the word attentive. I think of this word because of all the ways we see evidence of it everywhere. We see it in the solar system and the placements of the planets because they never collide, and Earth is placed so perfectly so that we do not burn or freeze. We can also see God's careful planning in our own bodies and how everything about us works and interacts with others. Only the most careful planning and thought could have made anything so precise.

Sometimes I wonder if God made some things just for fun if He was bored. The Fibonacci Sequence is one of those things because it is in so many things, even our hair, that it seems like it does not do anything except be there. Lots of times we take God's planning for granted, but if it wasn't for Him, we would not be here. If He did not pay attention, then we would not be as well off as we are. God is the most attentive being there is, and I am so glad that He is our Creator.

Giving God Our Anxiety
~ Sienna Duffield ~

Many people have things they are anxious about: a test that is coming up, a sick family member, or even asking that special someone out. The current world is filled with anxiety and stress, but we need to remember that God is in control. Many times, I will get overwhelmed about every little thing and forget that we have an amazing God on our side. I have had sleepless nights stressing and then finally remembered to read the Bible or say a prayer, and every time I do my mind can finally rest.

We often forget that a simple prayer will do incredible things in our lives. Many things can help with anxiety: telling a friend or trusted adult about it, walking in nature, and reading the Bible are all ways God can help you. Satan makes us want to keep our anxiety and continue to be uncertain, but if we surrender it to God, amazing things can happen. In current times everything seems uncertain. Will I go to school tomorrow? Will an important interview go well? Will COVID-19 finally be gone? We need to trust that God will take care of it. *"An anxious heart weighs a man down, but a kind word cheers him up"* (Proverbs 12:25, NIV).

Question of Faith
~ Eddie Dunfield ~

What is faith? Is it anything more than just believing? When people think of faith, they often come to the conclusion that faith is just the blind belief in God. Psalm 46:10 says, *"Be still and know that I am God. I will be exalted among the nations; I will be exalted in the earth!"* Faith is not just belief; it is more concrete and powerful. It is comparable to knowledge.

Daniel was not ready to be thrown into the lion's den just because he believed there was a God. He was sure of it. It was not just belief for him; he was completely certain with his trust in God. Daniel's faith was concrete; he was as sure about God as he was about himself.

When things get hard for us and we feel like our lives are falling apart, it is important to stay true to God. And if you feel your faith starts to waver, just remember that God will never put us through anything that we cannot handle. Faith is the conviction that what you believe, though it may not be backed up by evidence, exists. It is by God that we have faith, and by faith in God that we are saved.

Felt Like Giving Up?
~ Grant Early ~

Have you ever felt like just giving up on your job, your schoolwork, or yourself? And once you give up, do you find yourself running off into the woods and crawling into a hole all bunched together while someone buries you because you couldn't take the stress or the pain?

Jesus was told that He would die for everyone's sin to give us all a chance to be saved. Through all the hate and loss that Jesus witnessed, He just felt like giving up, wondering if He was truly good enough. But Jesus never gave up: He put his faith in God and never failed.

When we have horrible times in our lives and feel that we should run away, remember to trust in God, and He will provide a way for you to get through it all. Never lose sight of Him for He has a plan for us all, and no matter how hard it is, never give up because God is always by your side.

Lying Is a Sin?
~ Gavin Edelmann ~

"God is not a man, that He should lie, nor a son of man, that He should repent. Has He said, and will He not do? Or has He spoken, and will He not make it good?" (Numbers 23:19).

As a child most of us were told not to lie for it is bad, but if I told you that lying is supported in many situations what would you think? A sin is classified as being selfish or only thinking about yourself, so lying to cover somebody else is not a sin, right? The only way to find out is to ask God and He will give the answer in time with signs. Someone who lies to not get in trouble is only thinking about themselves. However, someone who lies and takes the blame for you is thinking about you. This is an act of random kindness in the heart whereas the other is an act of self-thought in the heart. Often, the reasons behind our actions are more important than the actions themselves.

The Leap of Faith
~ Hailey Fischer ~

"For he will command his angels concerning you to guard you in all your ways; they will lift you up in their hands, so that you will not strike your foot against a stone" (Psalm 91:11-12).

I slowly inched closer to the edge, hoping to catch a view from the top of the world. Step after step I took, until I could finally see the target 855 feet below me. But as I looked down, I realized that I was no longer afraid. Counting to three, I held my breath, and jumped.

Three hours earlier, I stood, looking up, at the giant in front of me. The Stratosphere in Las Vegas is one of the tallest buildings in the world and I was going to jump from the top. But I began to doubt myself and the cables that would support me. An endless stream of "What ifs" flowed through my head. What if the cables would not hold me and I would fall to my death? Eight hundred fifty-five feet could easily kill me. What if the wind picked up and I was blown against the tower? What if… What if…

Eventually, I got so nervous that I started shaking as I walked towards the elevator. Taking a deep, calming breath, I folded my hands and began praying. During my prayer, I decided that this jump would be my test of faith. God would send His guardian angels to protect me from striking my foot against the stone, or in my case dying on the pavement below. All I needed to do was trust Him. So, when I stood on that platform, I was not afraid. On that count of three, I leaped off and slowly fell to the ground, landing safely on the platform below.

God's Work
~ Cassie Fleck ~

Do you ever think what would happen if something in your life occurred differently because you made a different decision? Some might say events are just fate; others might say they are God's work. Well, in my story, I believe it to be God's work.

I was about seven years old when my dad first brought life changing news to our family back when I lived in Idaho. He announced that we were moving to the island of Guam. My heart saddened. I was young, had my friends and family, and went to school in Idaho . . . not Guam. I was furious with my parents for a long period of time till we moved to the island.

The first day on Guam, I pretended I hated it, but deep down I was having the time of my life on that little island. Fast forward two years. There I was, standing by the beach watching the waves crash. Standing there, I remembered of one of my favorite Bible texts, *"Wild waves of the sea, casting up their own shame like foam; wandering stars, for whom the black darkness has been reserved forever"* (Jude 1:13).

Looking back, I wish I could have trusted my parents when they said the move was the right decision, and, most importantly, I should have trusted God. Being on that island for two years made me see the incredible creations of God. I still look back and am so grateful for the memories I made there and the experiences I had. When you are at your lowest and feel like no one's there, trust in God. It's worth it.

Lighting the Way
~ Sidney Folkenberg ~

One thousand, one hundred and forty-six miles away from home. How could I leave the school I'd gone to since preschool and all my friends behind? How would I make new friends? What did God want me to do? Many questions filled my mind, and most of them I didn't have answers to. So, I prayed and prayed. I decided to go. Yes, I still had many doubts, but I didn't want the "what if" stuck in my brain for the rest of my life.

The time came to pack, leave home, and start the journey to UCA. There was no turning back now. After twelve hours of my dad driving, I took the wheel. I was driving up, over, and down mountains with darkness all around. I had no idea where I was. The only direction I had was a voice on my GPS telling me where to go and when to turn. My mind kept wandering. Did I make the right decision? Was this where God wanted me to be? Was this His plan for me, or did I mess it all up and choose the wrong path? My mind was flooded with these thoughts as the car drowned in the depths of darkness.

I looked up and on the side of a hill in the distance was a cross. Blackness was all around, yet there it was lighting the way. It reassured me this was the way I needed to go for God, and I had chosen right. It gave me hope and comfort. I don't know why God brought me here, and I'm still waiting to find out. If you're seeking guidance, ask Him for it. He might not give you a bright cross on a hill, but He will guide you until you find your path.

David and Goliath
~ Joshua Ford ~

We all have giants that we have to face in our lives, and that is where I think of the story of David and Goliath. David was a normal person who had to face giants or issues that would come up in his life. The story inspires me to think that whenever I am facing a giant in my life, I have a bigger giant on my side to help me through. When David was fighting Goliath, he only had a sling to fight the giant. When we are going through trouble, we feel so overwhelmed that we can't get through it, and we have nothing to defend ourselves. What we do not always realize is that God is always on our side, and that we also have the Bible to fight our giants.

"David said to the Philistine, 'You come against me with sword and spear and javelin, but I come against you in the name of the Lord Almighty, the God of the armies of Israel, whom you have defied" (1 Samuel 17:45).

Just a Bit Too Ambitious
~ Rachel Forrester ~

A while ago, when I first got my horse, I was a bit too ambitious for my own good. I was told to start slowly and walk her around the first few times. But as someone relatively new to horses, I did not know this was something serious. I was told to walk her the first 30-ish rides, but why do that when I could get on and race around like a car on an open highway? So, as you can probably already guess, I didn't warm up with a walk at all and went straight to a nice trot—although it was not nice at all! I was bucked off after about two minutes of "trotting"! I did not learn my lesson the first time and decided I would hop back on and go again. After speeding up for the second time (because being bucked off my horse once was not enough) I was bucked off that time, too. This one hit me HARD! After that, I fell into the biggest hole of fear I have ever been in during my lifetime. I did not ride my own horse for months. It was extremely tough for me and my trust in her was completely shattered. Little did I know that getting through that would turn out to be the biggest pivotal point in my life and my relationship with God. Since that day, about three years ago, I have continued to struggle with new things. My trust that God will guide me through, has been the only thing holding me to my faith.

Listen and Pray
~ Andrea Fowler ~

I believe God talks to us. Sometimes it's so quietly, you can barely hear, but other times it's so loud that you cannot hear anything else. My life experiences have taught me to listen whenever God speaks.

One of those experiences was on April 1, 2016. The night before, my parents and I were getting ready to make the four-hour long trip home after visiting my sisters at boarding school. When we were finally ready to leave, we reluctantly started saying our goodbyes. I hugged my oldest sister, Shiana, and then walked over to my second oldest sister, Julia, to say bye. We hugged each other tightly and gave each other words of love and encouragement. It was always so difficult to leave my sisters there. As I looked into her face with tears of sadness in my eyes, it felt surreal-like a scene from a movie. And in the back of my mind, I thought to myself, "This is the last time I will ever see her." That was the most terrifying thought I have ever had, that I might lose my best friend and biggest role model.

When we got into the car and started driving, I told my parents how I felt and started crying uncontrollably. My parents decided to pull over to the side of the road so we could pray about it. We prayed for a while then continued towards home. The next morning after driving home, we received a call from my sister's school saying that Julia had been in a bicycle accident and ripped open her knee. She was in the ER being numbed and stitched up. She had almost ridden off a cliff without wearing a helmet. She and a friend had been going down a steep hill and could not make a turn in the road. They crashed into each other and my sister cut open her knee. She could have died that day. I believe God impressed me to pray, and He answered my prayers. Never take for granted the time you get with loved ones. And listen when God tells you something.

Giving God Every Decision
~ Luke Ganson ~

Something I struggle with in my life is giving others control. It scares me not to know what is going to happen and to let another decide what is best for me. However, I need to let God oversee making the big decisions in my life. Many people base decisions on how they feel at the time and later they want a change or they give up. Proverbs 16:9 says, *"The heart of a man plans his ways, but the Lord establishes his steps."* Our hearts tell us what we desire, but we need to commit ourselves to God and let Him set our path for the journey ahead.

This summer my parents told me I could come to UCA if I wanted to. I told myself I would never come here because I had all my friends and life set up at home. I did not know a single soul here and knew nothing really about the school or even what it looked like. Although I knew in my heart that I did not want to, I decided to pray and ask God for guidance on what to do. Every single time I prayed, God made it very clear that He wanted me to go to UCA. There was such a strong conviction to go that I knew it must be God's leading in my life that made me feel that way.

My time here at UCA so far has been nothing but a blessing and a life-changing experience. The opportunities to make new friends, participate in spiritual activities, and even to play sports have blessed my life in more ways than I can count. When I look back, I realize if I had not given myself a chance to listen to God's voice, I would not be here at this school today. This has taught me to let God lead with every decision I make because He might have a better plan that I do not see.

I Am Enough
~ Aubrey Glover ~

Being "chosen" is always a big thing, whether it is for a sport's team, a group project or . . . anything. In most cases, we are chosen because of our special traits or abilities. Everyone wishes to be chosen for something at some point in their lives.

For me, being chosen has always been important. I struggle with knowing if I am good enough and if anyone will ever want me. Not too many people know that I am adopted. I was blessed to be chosen by my great aunt and uncle, but a part of me remembers the fact that my own biological parents didn't choose me, and if they didn't, then who else would?

In Ephesians 1:4 we read, *"Even before He made the world, God loved us and chose us in Christ to be holy and without fault in His eyes."* Being chosen by God isn't something we have to work for. God chose us exactly as we are and loves us just as we are. Each of us is chosen—without question. Knowing that I am loved and chosen and that there are no requirements I have to meet first means everything to me and reminds me that I am enough. And so are you.

Foggy Glasses
~ Byron Goertzen ~

"I will lead the blind by ways they've not known, along unfamiliar paths I'll guide them; I'll turn the darkness into light before them and make the rough places smooth. I won't forsake them" (Isaiah 42:16).

Everyone with glasses knows of the absolute loss of vision when one's glasses fog up. It may be when you open the dishwasher and all the steam fogs them, or when you're wearing a face mask and every time you breathe it sends a big cloud into your vision assistants, so you put the bridge over the nose piece, and it works for the first 10 minutes until they fog up again. The frustration is agonizing.

I was up at the popular ski resort, Schweitzer. It was so bitterly cold that when I breathed, my glasses would fog up to the point where I was blinder than a mole rat. I didn't think it was worth taking them off since I'm blind in a different way with them off, and I knew the hill decently well, so I started my way down "The Great Divide" and my glasses completely clouded over. I went careening straight off the side of the slope—which was quite the wake up! Where I went off, there was a cliff that went straight down into thick trees. But God was watching over me. I fell onto a small outcropping off the side of the cliff. I joked about it to my friends once I got back down the mountain, as adolescents do, but to this day I am very thankful that I avoided injury. When you are blinded by sin, you may find yourself waltzing straight off the side of a cliff. But God will catch you, even if you fall part of way the down.

Disappointments
~ Emely Guerrero ~

My father has a terrible singing voice. However, his lack of vocal talent did not stop him from doing a lot of singing for my brother and me. Although most of the songs he sang were children's Christian songs, there were two specific songs that he frequently sang to us: "Puff the Magic Dragon" and "The Country That I do Not Remember." Both of those songs spoke of the loss of innocence and life's disappointment, things that we experience as we grow older.

Disappointment is a sad reality of our lives, something we will experience daily—from the moment we realize that our parents are not perfect to when we see our own faults.

One misconception that exists in those who are coming to Christ is that they will face no disappointments in their Christian walk; however, the reality of the matter is that when Christ dwells in our hearts, it becomes easier to handle life's disappointments, but they will not disappear. The words of the hymn "Be Still My Soul" can help us understand how we should handle disappointment.

Be still my soul the Lord is on thy side
Bear patiently the cross of grief or pain
Leave to thy God to order and provide
In every change He faithful will remain
Be still my soul thy best, thy heavenly friend
Through thorny ways leads to a joyful end

Be still, my soul, thy God doth undertake
To guide the future as He has the past
Thy hope, thy confidence let nothing shake
All now mysterious shall be bright at last
Be still, my soul, the waves and winds still know
His voice who ruled them while He dwelt below

(Katharina Amalia Dorothea von Schlegel)

Real Love
~ Carly Haeger ~

"Set me as a seal upon your heart, as a seal upon your arm, for love is strong as death…" (Song of Solomon 8:6).

My junior year at UCA was my first year in Choraliers and in the Vocal Octet. Anyone who sang in these groups or heard us sing that year will recognize the verse above. This verse comprises the lyrics to a song the Choraliers and Octet sang. At first, I was indifferent to it; that was all it was—just a song that we sang. But throughout the school year, I began to love the words more and more. The song says this:

Set me as a seal upon your heart, as a seal upon your arm, for love is strong as death; Many waters cannot quench love, neither can the floods drown it.

This song reminds me of how enormous, how vast, how unending God's love is toward us. There is no way for us to wrap our minds around the expanse. We, as humans, want to be secure, to know without doubt that we are loved. This verse in Song of Solomon is of a young woman asking to be secure in the love of her beloved, *as a seal upon his heart.* A seal, a promise of love, pressed on his heart, where he will always remember it.

People who promise us love can let us down. It's easy to find an example of love that didn't last. But whenever I sing this song, I know without doubt that God loves me. There is nothing that can make Him forget me. As his child, I am secure, set as a seal upon His heart, for His love is *stronger* than death.

God's Fiery Mountain
~ Jonathan Haeger ~

It was 7:00 P.M. on Friday, September 11, 2020. The fire was slowly moving across the mountain, taking its time. Then it changed. Fast. Wind picked up and the fire sped across the hillside moving more in 20 minutes than it had in the past two days. As the fire moved, it threw embers across a highway into a game reserve that stretched into our neighborhood. Nobody knew what the fire would do. The game reserve was dry since it hadn't rained in a long time. After seeing that the fire was in the reserve, we decided to go home and prepare for the worst. We moved some personal items and our boat to a friend's house. We put up ladders to each of the roofs in our neighborhood planning to take hoses up and put out any embers that fell on them. We were the only ones there. Eventually, we realized the fire wasn't doing much, so we decided to go to bed. Waking up the next morning, we discovered that we were completely out of danger.

Satan works like that fire. If you are in a relationship with God, Satan is going to target you, and if he can get a seed of doubt in you, he can take you and rip you away from where you were. He can take you to where all hope seems lost. God doesn't always stop the fire but will continue to be with us during the fire. Sometimes He sees fit to stop the fire; sometimes He holds us in His hand while the fire burns. Either way, we can be sure of His protection and love.

Don't Let Disappointment Get You Down
~ Genevieve Harbour ~

Have you ever dealt with disappointments in your life? Well this year I have dealt with many things that have made me disappointed. At the beginning of this year when I heard about COVID-19, I did not think it would be much, until we all had to be sent home. The main thing that really hit me with disappointment was not being able to go on the Spain trip. About a year before I started going to UCA my family had told me that on spring break of my freshman year I would be going to Spain and Portugal. I have never been out of North America and I was so excited to see something new. Then COVID-19 hit hard, and we canceled the trip completely. I was so upset. In situations like these all we can do is pray to God and trust His plan.

In Psalm 62:8 it says, *"Trust in Him at all times, oh people; pour out your heart before Him; God is a refuge for us."* I believe this verse is perfect for that time when I just needed to trust God. That verse says always trust in Him, which is something we always need to do. So, don't let one thing that has made you disappointed get you down. Always trust in God that things will work out for the better.

Just Keep Loving
~ Lorelei Harbour ~

In the Bible, it is clear to see that the overarching theme is love. We see it again and again throughout the chapters and amid the stories. Verses tell us of God's love for us, the golden rule tells us to love our neighbor, and a whole chapter in 1 Corinthians is dedicated to the subject. To love might seem a simple task, but it is a lot harder than one might expect. To love means being happy for your friend when you find out that they made a team or group that you did not. It means learning to let go of grudges and forgiving those who have hurt you. It means being there for your archnemesis when their favorite hamster dies, rather than thinking to yourself, "Ha. It's what she deserved."

"Love is patient, love is kind..." 1 Corinthians 13 gives us an outline of what love looks like. It tells us that you could rise to be the greatest president America has ever seen or be full of so much faith in God that you could move mountains; but without love, you are absolutely nothing. Love is the greatest language anyone can learn to speak, and it will last forever. Sometimes, we have days when showing love is like passing pre-calculus with 100%--basically impossible. Yes, we are sinful beings who cannot love perfectly, but that is no excuse not to try at all. In order to get started, I recommend a prayer that I try to say every day. Ask God to live through you and to help you live out love. I am far from perfect, and I make mistakes, but love has changed my life. It has opened my eyes to the beauty in everyone around me and has, overall, made me a truly happier person. So I encourage you to just let go and love.

"Three things will last forever – faith, hope, and love – and the greatest of these is love" (1 Corinthians 13:13).

Drowning
~ Levi Hardy ~

"The engulfing waters threatened me… To the roots of the mountains I sank down; the earth beneath barred me in forever. But you, Lord my God, brought my life up from the pit" (Jonah 2:5-6).

When I was nine, I went to the beach. I didn't know it that morning, but there were strong riptides underneath the calm sea. I went swimming in the water with my cousins and brother. I jumped into a big wave, and when I popped up from the water, I realized I was being sucked out to sea. I began to thrash around, shouting at my uncle and dad to save me, but my voice was completely blocked by the noise of the waves.

As I struggled against the waves, I began to swallow water, and I could not help thinking about how deep the ocean was and wondering what was under me. This made me thrash around even more. All my efforts to get back to shore were not helping, and with every swell that came through I swallowed more water. My lungs hurt; my body felt weak. This did not help me or get me any closer to shore. It was then that I believed I was going to drown. When I turned my body around, trying to see the shore, I saw the lifeguard had finally seen me and was coming to get me. He grabbed me, and swimming long strokes, he dragged me back to the beach. It took me a few days to go swimming again, but I did, and that has never happened again.

When we are drowning in today's troubles and problems, God is there even if He does not save us right away. He will not let you die, and He will save you. He will come grab you and drag you back to the beach of safety.

Eyes on the Prize
~ Logan Henneberg ~

During the middle of summer, my family decided to go dirt biking. We went to one of my dad's favorite areas to ride because of this one trail. We rode around a bit as a family on a separate trail for a few hours. It was fun, but I was ready for more. We rode back to our truck and my mom and brother decided to stay while my dad and I took on the steep trail with many rocks. In order to get to it, we had to ride through foot-high water—which doesn't seem like a lot until you're on a bike. We ascended the trail while trying not to fall off the edge. Along the way, we encountered jumps and the occasional side-by-side. It was great! We reached the top, admired the view, and turned around. First off, it's important to know that I prefer going up steep trails to going down; second, I recently had gotten a new Kawasaki KLX 300, which is a big bike. So I was taking my time, avoiding rocks and taking jumps slowly. I constantly had my eyes on the trail. Until I didn't. I looked away for what felt like only a second, when a stone popped up out of nowhere and I hit it. When I hit the stone, my feet launched up, kicking myself out of gear. My bike slammed to a stop after sliding a few feet. I crashed to the side with my feet dangling off the edge. However, I was okay in the end.

I believe that the moral to my story is to keep your eyes on Jesus. He will protect you if you follow His path, just like I was safe as long as I kept my eyes on the prize: Jesus.

God at Work
~ Alex Hermanson ~

This story shows how God works in our lives. My grandfather had been sent overseas and was staying on his ship in Korea. When they arrived at a port, they were given time off, so a group of them went out to see the city. A lot of them bought cameras and binoculars because they were inexpensive, being that Korea was the place where they were manufactured. When night came my grandfather told his group that he was going to head back to the ship. The rest wanted to stay out longer to get a drink. When they heard he was heading back, they all asked him to take their cameras and binoculars back to the ship for them. He said he would, so he placed a great assortment of cameras and binoculars around his neck.

While he was walking, two women came out of a building and pulled him into a closet, speaking to him in Korean. Not understanding what they were saying, he knew they were doing something important by the tone of their voices, so he stayed in the closet and was quiet. After a while they let him out and he headed back to the ship.

The next morning, my grandfather's friends all came to get their items. "Did you get stopped by the police?" they asked. Then his friends told him that the police were stopping people because of a thief. If he had been seen with all their cameras and binoculars around his neck without any proof of purchase, he would have been put in jail. God kept him safe and had the two women hide him while they were looking for the thief. This shows how God keeps us safe every day and watches over us.

Blind from Birth
~ Matt Hermanson ~

How would you feel if you could not see? A lot of people might be scared, while others are experiencing this right now. The star-nosed mole is born blind. Star-nosed moles see the world with their nose; their noses look like a star, with twenty-two appendages, and each has twenty-five thousand sensory organs on the surface. The moles live their lives without seeing one inch in front of their nose, yet this does not stop the star-nosed mole from digging miles of tunnels in its lifetime. Not only do the moles hunt in their tunnels, but they also search nearby ponds and wetlands for prey.

Star-nosed moles cannot see what is in front of them, but are they scared? No! They take life one step at a time and focus on what is happening. We sometimes focus on the future and what is going to happen but forget to live in the present. If you trust in God, He will guide your life and protect you.

"'For I know the plans I have for you,' declares the Lord, 'plans to prosper you and not to harm you, plans to give you hope and a future'"
(Jeremiah 29:11).

Serving Others
~ Mayah Hernandez ~

"In the same way, let your light shine before others, that they may see your good deeds glorifying your Father in heaven" (Matthew 5:16).

A few days before Thanksgiving our class went on a trip to the food bank. Many of us did not want to go because we were tired from the long day before. We went along anyways, in a cold bus in the morning, wrapping ourselves in clothing. When we got there, they went through the main idea and how the whole point of today was to package potatoes and apples. The job was easy, but not all the potatoes were in the best shape. They were rotten, porridge looking, and made my stomach turn, but I still picked them up and threw them away.

I went out and saw a line of people going around through the aisles, happily talking with each other and enjoying their time there shopping for their Thanksgiving meal. I felt better, and although I was still a little tired, it was a good experience. In Philippians 2:4 it says, *"Not looking to your own interests but each of you to the interests of the others."* In the end when you help others you will feel better about yourself and others.

Clothe Yourselves with Compassion
~ William Heyden-Seaton ~

Did you know that humpback whales spread and copy songs that get popular? Humpback whales in the South Pacific follow music trends based on the season, which then always spread from west to east over the span of a year or two.

We humans also do this after a fashion. When someone writes a song that a lot of people like, it spreads throughout our culture. These songs also influence the type of music we then like or think is cool.

But songs are not the only things that spread and have influence. The way you act also influences the people around you. This is why we should always act like Jesus and be kind to people. The way you act can affect them too. If you are being rude and terse then it could spread and put someone else in a bad mood. But if you are kind to them then you could make their day better.

As Colossians 3:12 says, *"Therefore, as God's chosen people, holy and dearly loved, clothe yourselves with compassion, kindness, humility, gentleness and patience."*

The Hit
– Ethan Hickok –

"Blessed is the man who remains steadfast under trial, for when he has stood the test, he will receive the crown of life, which God has promised to those who love him" (James 1:12).

It was a young morning in Tallahassee, Florida. The ground was wet, and the team was ready. It was my first cross-country nationals. The gun was about to go off and I prayed for the Lord to help me in the race, knowing whatever happened that He would get me through. BAAM! We were off, and at a faster pace than I was comfortable with. I slowed down to the back of the second pack. A third of the way into the race I was feeling good and started to pick up my pace. By the halfway point I had gotten to the front of the second pack, meaning I was pacing them. I slowly sped up as one person at a time dropped off. It was three other people and me. One of them tried to pass me, but I quickly pulled in front of him and he pulled back. We went through this routine a few more times and then it was just us. In between the first and second pack, I ran on the inside as we came around a turn. The other guy quickly jumped in front of me and shouldered me into the rebar that was holding up the course ropes. I gasped in pain as the air left my body, but I continued to run. I had significantly slowed down by then and the blood oozing down my back was not making it easier. I was about 200 meters behind the person who shouldered me, and there was about a half mile left in the race. I picked up my pace. I kept my eyes locked on my target as I came closer to it. There were 500m left in the race and I was 50m behind my target. At 200m I started my kick. I was just feet behind him, sprinting fast as I dove for the finish. After I recovered, I looked at the scoreboard, discovering my defeat. I went back to my tent in pity, sad about my finish. When we went out for awards, they listed off all the disqualifications like always. I looked at the scoreboard again, and from 101st place my name moved to 100! The guy who had elbowed me was disqualified! I heard the announcer say that a spectator saw an athlete purposefully shove another athlete. My team celebrated with me for getting top 100. I went to the med tent for a towel because I was bleeding. I remembered my prayer from the start of the race, and I knew that God had been there for me.

Which Path?
~ Owen Hickok ~

"You can enter God's Kingdom only through the narrow gate. The highway to hell is broad, and its gate is wide for the many who choose that way. But the gateway to life is very narrow and the road is difficult, and only a few ever find it" (Matthew 7:13-14).

I once went mountain biking with some friends up at Schweitzer Mountain. It was an amazing and sunny day; the clouds were gone, and the trees were swaying. I looked over the path I was going to take, and it had this extraordinary, huge jump. I was in the back of the group because I tend to fall, but we started to go down and we were flying! We came to the big jump; one after another, everyone else went off it. There was a trail to skip the jump, and something told me to skip it, but I decided I wanted to hit it. It was finally here; I went up and as I was coming down, I landed too far forward and flew over my handlebars. I fell off the trail and I slid on rocks and branches 50 feet down. I got back up after a few minutes with blood on my face and arms.

There are going to be two paths in life, and you can choose which one you want to go down. There is the righteous path or the dark, sinful path. Trust me, you want to go down the path with Jesus, not the one with Satan. Your life is going to be full of awesome and awful surprises, but no matter how hard life is, always follow the way of God. He will always keep you on the right path; He will never let you fall off the trail.

Busy? "Text me when ur done"
~ Carson Huenergardt ~

People are texting pretty much every day at every second. Eighty-seven percent of teens sleep with their phones by them just in case they get that must-read text. According to a study, the average teen will send at least 100 texts a day.

Most teens would rather text than any other method of communication. It's easy, it's private, and it's more comfortable than a face-to-face conversation would be. Teens like it for the instant feedback as well. Every time you send a text you expect an immediate response. What if we thought the same way about God: the moment we pray we want an instant answer? If everyone expected God to give us a direct and instantaneous response, we would probably lose faith because we wouldn't give God enough time to work. What if we read our Bible and studied the ways of Jesus as much as we used our phones? Using smart phones to communicate with our friends and family is not a bad thing, but when it gets in the way of praising and worshiping Jesus, then it becomes an idol. If you take and spend time with Him every day, you will eventually hear His voice finding its way into your life.

"Be careful for nothing; but in everything by prayer and supplication with thanksgiving let your requests be made known unto God" (Philippians 4:6).

The Love of God
~ Ryan Hughes ~

Have you ever been mad at someone? I am sure that you have. I know it has happened to me. We all get upset at someone one time or another. It is in our sinful nature to become agitated or angry at those around us. The reasons may seem justified, but does that matter? God sent His only Son, Jesus, to us. Why would we be worth saving?

It seems God should be mad at our human race, but He is a God of love. The concept of perfect love is so foreign to us we can only catch fleeting glimpses of it. This world has been corrupted, but the great news is that we do not have to go down with this world! We have our Rescuer who loves us to an incomprehensible level. This love has such power; it truly is our most powerful tool.

We often get caught up thinking about what they did, what they said, and what they still do. Tangled in this trap of valuing people based on their deeds, we lose sight of what matters. What matters is love. How great would this world be if we all prioritized loving and helping others? What if we spent more time loving, and less time judging? Next time you want to judge people for what they did, think of love. God has given us love, and as Christians what should stop us from sharing? Nothing!

The Siberian Tiger
~ Nathanael Hunton ~

The Siberian tiger is one of my favorite examples of why God created everything and designed it perfectly. I will tell you why. First of all, the Siberian tiger is the largest of its species, weighing in at an averaging of around 300kg (600lbs), with an average length of 70 inches from its head to the end of its tail. The Siberian tiger can even reach speeds of 90kph (60mph), and it can run at that speed in snow. Because of all of those expert designs, the Siberian tiger can thrive in its habitat and is known as the top predator with very few difficulties except for human hunting and deforestation.

All in all, the lesson you should take away from this is that if we let Jesus in, we will be more equipped for our spiritual and real life. In addition, we will be protected from the harm caused by Satan and will soon see our Lord in heaven.

You Can't Control Everything
~ Whitni Johansen ~

People need to trust God has the best intentions. I was forced to come to UCA and was trying to tell my parents not to bring me here. I tried everything not to come. When they told me that I was coming anyway, I hated them for bringing me here even though I had repeatedly told them I did not want to. But, eventually, I started to like it. And going to this school soon became an awesome experience.

Quite a few of people try to control everything and want things their own way. That is not always best for you because when God tries to guide you in your decisions, and you want to control your own way, there will be consequences. Sometimes God will allow us to learn hard lessons. Sometimes you just need to relax and have faith that your life and situation will work out. Let go a little and just let life happen instead of trying to control everything.

"Do not let your heart be troubled, believe in God, believe also in Me" (John 14:1).

God's Purpose for People
~ Jordan Johns ~

Sometimes, people wonder what God's plan is for them. The Bible says that God's plans for us are for our welfare and they will give us a future and a hope (Jeremiah 29:11). God cannot lie, so we know that the promises He made in the Bible are still being carried out today in the present. This is a great promise of God because it helps you know that your life is in God's hands and if you diligently seek Him, He will reward you.

You might ask, how do I know God is telling the truth? I know that God is telling the truth because He is the Most Holy, and if He lies, He would be imperfect, and not holy. Therefore, we should not worry about God not telling the truth. We should have faith in God and let Him guide us through our difficulties.

People may think that God does not have a purpose for them, or they will not be saved, but we know that God has incredible plans for us, and we will have a bright future with God.

"For by grace you have been saved through faith, and that not of yourselves, it is the gift of God" (Ephesians 2:8).

Whom Do You Choose?
~ Tori Johnson ~

Going into freshman year I didn't know who I was, and honestly, I still don't. Everyone around me was trying so hard to fit in. It was all kind of a blur. I was always surrounded by people, but I never felt like anyone really knew me. Being there for people was always important to me, but at the end of the day who was there for me?

All of a sudden, our year was cut short and we were thrown into quarantine. No longer surrounded by people, I was left with myself. Being locked away from society shows you who you really are. I don't know about you, but quarantine helped me become who I am today.

For me this year is all about making friends, memories, and cherishing the time we have together. You never know when your year might be cut short. It's all about lifting people up and choosing to be there for people instead of judging them. I've always had trouble feeling like I fit in with people. This year, for the first time, I feel like I'm starting to find a few people who would choose to be there for me in the same way I'd choose to be there for them. Now, I am not saying the struggle is over, but if you ever struggle with anything just remember God supports you and chooses you every day. No matter how much you push Him away He's still got your back.

The Dirt Bike
~ Skyla Jordan ~

When I was younger, my parents introduced me to dirt biking. For my birthday, they got me a tiny Yamaha. Every day after school, I would go to a small field down the road and ride until the sun went down. Being only five years old, I would have to go with a parent every time. However, one day I decided that I was old enough to go by myself.

As quietly as I could, I took my dirt bike from the garage and rode to the field. As time went on, I was doing great; I had not fallen once. I got a little cocky and eyed the small jump we had made. Without hesitation, I lined myself up with it and cranked back the throttle. Once in the air, I realized the mistake I had made. I had never done a jump before; I had no idea what I was doing. The next thing I knew, I was on the ground with the bike on top of me. My dad ran up, seemingly out of nowhere, picked up the dirt bike, and helped me back home. I was expecting him to be upset at me for leaving, but to my surprise, he was anything but that. He only cared that I was okay.

God is the same way. Although we may think that we are strong enough to make our own decisions, God will always be there when we need Him. He does not hold a grudge but instead rejoices in the fact that we are home. Like Zephaniah 3:17 says, *"The Lord your God is with you, the Mighty Warrior who saves. He will take great delight in you; in His love He will no longer rebuke you but will rejoice over you with singing."*

The Guardian Angel
~ Jonathan Kasper ~

"The angel of the Lord encamps around those who fear Him, and He delivers them" (Psalm 34:7).

What do you think of when you hear the word "Alaska?" Many people underestimate the true beauty of Alaska. While it does have ice in the far north and gets cold in the winter, the many forests and national parks show that Alaska is not just about cold. I lived in Alaska for four and a half years. I experienced hot summers and cold winters, but nothing compared to what happened on our move to Texas.

When we entered Canada, we encountered a bad blizzard. There had been many reports of accidents caused by slippery roads, and the falling snow was so thick that it was difficult to see anything ahead.

Since we could barely see, it would be impossible to stop if we came across a bad accident. As we were driving, trying to get ahead of the storm, we saw the blinking lights of a semi-truck in front of us. We slowly followed the lights down the road. Suddenly, the truck moved over to the other lane. Not knowing what to do, we followed it. Shortly after, we saw many cars crashed on the side of the road under a bridge.

This experience reminds me of Psalm 34:7, where David reminds us that God is always watching over us and sends his guardian angels to protect us. We have no doubt that the semi-truck driver was an angel because it guided us away from the trouble. God will always protect you no matter what kind of situation you are in. Trust Him and He will send His guardian angels to protect you from danger and all the troubles and traps of the devil.

The Difference
~ Caitlin Krause ~

How can I make a difference as a Christian? The story that best illustrates this to me is *The Starfish Story* by Loren Eisley. In her story, a man is walking on the beach when he sees a young boy throwing things into the water, taking a few steps and repeating. The man asks the boy what he is doing, to which the boy replies, "I'm saving these starfish that are stranded. If they stay on the beach they will dry out and die, so I'm putting them back into the ocean so they can live."

"Young man," the man said, "on this stretch of beach alone there must be more than a hundred stranded starfish. Around the next corner, there must be at least a thousand more. This goes on for miles and miles. I've done this walk every day for ten years, and it's always the same. There must be millions of stranded starfish! I hate to say it, but you'll never make a difference."

The boy replies, "Well I just made a difference for that one," and continues with his work.

I believe that God put us here for a reason, even if that reason is just to tell one person about His love. Then you too could say you made a difference for that one. That might seem insignificant, but that one person you told may end up preaching to nations, and that would never have happened without you introducing them to Jesus. Now your "small" difference will not seem so small anymore.

"Before I formed you in the womb I knew you, before you were born I set you apart; I appointed you as a prophet to the nations" (Jeremiah 1:5).

Trust
~ Abby Kriger ~

"Trust in the Lord with all your heart and lean not on your own understanding; in all your ways submit to Him, and He will make your paths straight" (Proverbs 3:5-6).

We all go through hardships in our life; some may be worse than others. I remember when I was younger something very tragic happened in my family. We all didn't know how we were going to get through this hardship, but we tried our best. We prayed and talked to God a lot more than we did before; we put all our trust in Him.

Later on I was talking to my mom and she told me, "You know what? If this hardship we faced a year or two ago didn't happen, would we be closer to God? Because of what happened we were able to spend more time with God and not be distracted all the time." Now I realize that all she said was true. We just have to trust in God and see where He takes us, even if we get scared or something tragic happens. Just trust the Lord our God for He is the Creator of the universe. What can we do that our God can't?

Chosen to go to UCA
~ Joseph Lee ~

When I first came to UCA, I was very nervous and scared. I did not want to come to UCA at first, but when I arrived and met the people here, I changed my mind.

Near the end of my eighth grade year, I had to think of what high school I wanted to attend. At first I wanted to go to the high school near my home where all my "friends" from middle-school were going to. Then, people kept talking to me about UCA and how great it was. I was very hesitant because it was in another state eight hours away. I did not want to go, but I still applied. I waited a week or so, and then I got an email telling me I got accepted. I then proceeded to pack and order things off Amazon. Package after package came to my doorstep; stacks of cardboard boxes began to pile up near my trash.

When the time came to go to UCA, I said bye to my closest friends and started my eight-hour drive to Spangle, Washington. When I finally arrived, I looked around and all I saw was a school in the middle of nowhere surrounded by wheat fields. When I walked into my dark and gloomy dorm room, I got even more hesitant. I moved all my belongings in and just took a deep breath. After my parents left, I remembered the Bible verse: *"Even though I walk through the darkest valley I will fear no evil, for You are with me; Your rod and Your staff comfort me"* (Psalms 23:4). I kept this near my heart and believed that God would protect me. After that I knew that I was chosen to come to UCA.

Come Follow Me
~ Ava Lennon ~

We are all disciples of Jesus Christ. We were made to spread the love and salvation of God all over the world. The day Jesus said to his disciples, "Come follow me!" our world changed. He told Peter, Andrew, and Simon to fish for people, and at once they dropped their nets and went to follow Him. At that moment, when they went to follow Him, they had no idea how many amazing miracles God would perform.

We are all sinners but when we choose to follow God, our lives will most definitely be changed in miraculous ways. I imagine what it would be like to meet God. I think I would have had the same reaction if He told me to come and follow Him. He is the person I've been praying to my entire life. Will you come and follow Him?

And He says to them, *"Come follow after Me, and I will make you fishers of men"* (Matthew 4:19).a

Protection
~ Alesia Levchenko ~

"For I know the plans I have for you, plans to prosper you and to not harm you, plans to give you hope and a future" (Jeremiah 29:11).

I was about 10, but I still remember making plans, packing our stuff, and heading out for the two-hour drive. We haven't gone camping in a long time and decided to go with another family. I was going to sleep in a tent!

We pulled up the ramp onto the highway and all of a sudden it felt like our car was sitting there and dust was everywhere outside the windows. The door on my brother's side was jammed and wouldn't open. I saw the stopped traffic, and another car was flipped.

Everything after that was pretty shocking. In the opposite lane, a man had been driving and talking on his phone, and his car went into the wrong lane. We almost had a head-on collision, but he lifted his head just in time to turn, hitting us on the side and flipping. My dad also swerved and we spun while he was trying to steady the car. The man was a little scratched up, but everyone in my family was completely unharmed.

About that time the other family called. They had some reason so that they couldn't go camping either, so we had our grandpa pick us up and drive us home.

The next day our friends called us. They said they watched the news and told us that there had been a terrible wind storm at the campsite where we would have camped that night. There was lightning and many trees fell. There were some fatalities. I feel like God really protected both of the families. Even though we might have had a broken-down car, we were ok, and didn't possibly die in the forest.

The Question
~ Tanner Lowe ~

Is God real? I have heard people ask this question a lot in my life, and I am only 15. In fact, I have asked myself this question. Going to a Christian school almost all my life, and especially UCA, has helped me answer this question. The spiritual presence on this campus has shaped my life in a great way. But there was a point in time where I had no idea where to go and what to do.

Last year I was in the Fall Classic soccer tournament. During the last game for first and second place, I fell over and messed up my hip. The pain kept growing, but I kept playing because I wanted to win the game. My position was right striker and we had to make some goals to catch up. Towards the end of the last half, I had to sit out because of pain. But I was not done. I did not want to sit out the rest of the game, so I told Coach I was okay. I went back in and I had the perfect opportunity to score. I believe that God gave me the strength to make the goal and push through.

God is real and does care about the little things in life and will see us through.

Synonymity of Happiness and Boredom
~ Asher Mack ~

We often brush off uninteresting moments and seemingly average activities (jobs, chores, school work) as negative parts of our lives. But here's the thing: Mundanity and the boredom of everyday life is an essential part to being a mentally happier person.

Have you thought about what happens when your sugar intake is high? Your affinity for sugary products and taste value goes down. When you heavily limit your sugar intake, however, the opposite happens. You find previously not-so-sweet things much sweeter.

I believe the same principle applies to emotional well-being. If your life is oversaturated with stimulating devices and moments, you will seek further distraction and stimulation to compensate for the decline in effectiveness. Smartphones, televisions, video games, almost all things virtual take away the excitement from our other experiences because they are so visually and verbally stimulating.

If, however, you limit your exposure to such things and seek out distractions less often, and, most importantly, **embrace** the boring and mundane, you will find that life will regain its lovely vibrance once again.

This is far from an argument against very mentally stimulating things. Occasional use is fine. Going back to the sugar metaphor, ice cream on weekends is not going to heavily affect the rest of the week. Find beauty not in things that are attractive to do, but things that are unattractive. Hike up a mountain. Catch up on dishes. Sit and think for 30 minutes instead of checking Twitter. Do this, and I promise you some of the color that life seemed to have lost will return to you.

Pride
~ Maddox Mack ~

Does God help us win in the things we do? Proverbs 16:18 states: *"Pride comes before the destruction."* So I believe that He lets us win when we are humble about it, but if we get too prideful about the things we win at, then there will be consequences for that. James 4:6 says, *"But He gives more grace."* Can pride be good in certain situations?

If we are humble in the things we win at, I believe God will allow us to continue to win with honor and a graceful heart. There was once an NBA player who won a championship in the previous season for his team. He then allowed pride in his heart and said, "There is no God, I am God." The next year he loses in the first round of the playoffs. The team sorrowfully separated, and no one ever talked to him since then.

Galatians 6:3 says, *"For if anyone thinks he is something, when he is nothing, he deceives himself."* Recently there has been more success in sports because many basketball players (and other athletes also) have been giving their lives and hearts to the Lord and staying true to their faith, and then they start to succeed in the aspects of the game they strive to be good at. Philippians 2:3 says, *"Do nothing from rivalry or conceit, but in humility count others more significant than yourselves."*

The Dog and the Paddleboard
~ Brynn Martsching ~

Last summer my family and I went to a lake and went paddle boarding. My dog loves to get on the paddle board with us, but she does not like to stay on for very long. I decided I wanted to take her to a peninsula the next bay, so I got her on the paddle board and started paddling. At first, she really liked it, but the farther away we got from shore, the more she kept whining. I didn't want to take her back, so I kept going. She didn't like that and jumped off. It was too far for her to swim to land or any place where she could rest, so she circled around me and whined. I pulled her back on to the board and went back to shore.

God tries to keep us close to Him, but sometimes we wander and get lost. But if we ask, He will pull us back to Him.

Chosen
~ Kyler McCombs ~

Being chosen for something feels great. It implies that you were needed or wanted. You were desired by someone else because of who you are. You were seen as important.

When God sees us, He sees something of infinite value and crucial importance. He looks at us with greater love and compassion than we could ever understand. He chose us; God chose you. Jesus paid a very high price for you so you could someday spend the rest of time with Him in a perfect place that He prepared. Each day, God chooses you, pursuing you to the ends of the earth, wanting desperately to give you the gift of eternal life. God has chosen you and continues to choose you every chance He gets. All God wants is a close relationship with you. He wants you to trust Him and to walk and talk with Him. God wants you. You are chosen.

Sometimes we don't feel like we should be chosen. We think we lack value or importance. We get so caught up in our daily routines and stresses that we forget who we are in God's eyes. Despite our many imperfections and the countless times we have fallen short, He still sees us as His beautiful creation, His child. God has already chosen you. In Deuteronomy 7:6, it says, *"For you are a people holy to the Lord your God. The Lord your God has chosen you out of all the peoples on the face of the earth to be his people, his treasured possession."* His decision has already been made. It's our turn to do what He has been longing for since before we were even conceived. We are chosen.

You Are Chosen
~ Hannah Mercill ~

God says He will always be with us no matter where we are, what we are doing, or what we are going through.

He says in Isaiah 43:1-2, *"Do not fear, for I have redeemed you; I have summoned you by name; you are mine. When you pass through the waters, I will be with you; and when you pass through the rivers, they will not sweep over you. When you walk through the fire, you will not be burned; the flames will not set you ablaze."*

This is only part of God's promise for us. He loves us so much He will do whatever we need to keep us safe. He will protect us from fire so that we will not be burned. He will even keep us from drowning.

Sometimes God does not protect us because He has something else He wants us to experience, something we can use to help someone else overcome their pain or loss.

You may feel He has, but God never leaves you. There are so many times where God does miracles; we are just too blind to see them or even notice because we are more worried about the little things that are not worth worrying about.

You may be chosen to experience a hardship or to feel pain so you might be able to help someone else through the pain they are going through. That was part of the deal when you signed up for eternal life. In the end it will all be worth it.

The Outcast of Freshman Year
~ Nathan Michael ~

What was my freshman year like? Well, I can tell you it was not the best year at all. It started off with being crippled for four months with a broken ankle. I didn't really have a lot of friends, and because of my ankle, I couldn't get out much to meet new people. My only friend was my roommate, Jake. I felt like I was an outcast, left out of everything. I felt lost and thought I had lost God.

Psalm 73:23-26 says, *"Yet I am always with you; you hold me by my right hand. You guide me with your counsel, and afterward you will take me into your glory. Whom have I in heaven but you? And earth has nothing I desire but you. My flesh and my heart may fail, but God is the strength of my heart and my portion forever."*

Do not make the same mistake I made. You are never alone. You always have someone there for you. God will always be there no matter the situation—through thick and thin. I had lost my way in life until God found me along the way. My life changed instantly, and my love for Him grew. I'm not alone anymore.

Even though you might feel out of place or separate from everyone else, there will always be someone there for you till the end of time. Pray to God and He will answer, for He loves you so very much.

Perfect Timing
~ Jaden Michaelis ~

"Commit to the Lord whatever you do, and He will establish your plans" (Proverbs 16:3). I'm one of those people who loves to exercise and to get stronger in many things. I love to work-out and to see how my body is improving. I had a very specific work-out that I started to do at the start of my eighth grade year. I kept to my work out for most of the school year. Then COVID-19 hit, and I stopped working out. I was stuck at home and wasn't motivated to do anything. All I did each day was do online classes, homework, and then absolutely nothing. I tried to exercise as much as I could, but that wasn't much. I felt like I was failing in life. I was doubting my worth in the world. Then I found the perfect story.

Each night, I read from a devotional book. The stories in this book are written by high schoolers so a lot of their stories are very relatable. One night, I was reading and came across a story called, "An Empty Heart" by Sydney Hoffman. That same night, I was worrying about my fitness and what I wanted in life. Sydney explained that we shouldn't be distracted from God with earthly things. God is the only one who can give you what you want. Now this really touched me and answered my silent prayer to God. It's like most pastors will say to you, "God will answer your prayer in a way you don't suspect."

Heart Attack
~ Jake Mitchell ~

December 21, 2019, Christmas Sabbath. My father goes to the stage and begins playing. The sweet melody of "Ave Maria" fills the sanctuary, a flawless performance. Soon after, my father returns to his seat next to my mother and me. The next performers come on to the stage, and I begin watching attentively. Soon, however, I notice my mother and father whispering, both seeming frantic. In an instant, I was told to grab my father's trumpet and rush to the car. My father had had a heart attack.

From church, we rushed to the nearest hospital, which was a mere five minutes away. After being evaluated, he was rushed into surgery and had multiple stents put in. As my family and I waited, terrified, word got out at church about the incident. Friends, family, and both of our pastors came to support us and pray with us.

After about two and a half hours, his surgery was done, and we could go see him. The doctors told us that his surgery had gone well. He would only have to stay in the hospital for a couple of days and would be home for Christmas. If my father had not been asked to play that day, we may not have made it to the hospital. We may not have been at church. From our home, the hospital is about 20 minutes away, but from our church, it is only five minutes. Being at church may have saved my father's life.

The Lord wants us to live full, abundant, and happy lives, and He will always be with us, watching over us and protecting us. Not only did He protect my father and allow him to be home for Christmas, but He also supported my family and me as we worried, sending friends, family, and pastors to be with us. *"When you pass through the waters, I will be with you; and when you pass through the rivers, they will not sweep over you. When you walk through the fire, you will not be burned; the flames will not set you ablaze"* (Isaiah 43:2).

You're Never Alone
~ Elijah Montes ~

As all of you should know COVID-19 has affected all of us in differing ways, whether that's your parents losing their jobs, or you not being able to eat in one of your favorite restaurants. On March 13, 2020 my high school was closed. Those who hadn't resided on campus were to go home, and dorm students awaited the bus and packed their clothes along with their thoughts. Most were overjoyed with the fact we had a "break" from school, and others were fearful of coming events. Upon the arrival at my home, I sat and realized what had just happened. It was shocking. I had no idea when I was going to see my friends again.

During such times, I often find myself thinking mournful thoughts. But right when I feel I'm alone and there's no hope, I pray. I find myself praying very often through these times, knowing I'm not alone and never losing hope for God is with me wherever I go. When dark and gloomy thoughts enter my mind, I always open my Bible and read through verses that give me hope. This gives me some sense of clarity that all will be fine and that God always has a plan for me and you. You must not lose an ounce of hope, for God is always with you.

"'For I know the plans I have for you,' declares the Lord, 'plans to prosper you and not to harm you, plans to give you hope and a future'" (Jeremiah 29:11).

The Lost Found Sheep
~ Faith Montes ~

"Doesn't he leave the ninety-nine in the open country and go after the lost sheep until he finds it? And when he finds it, he joyfully puts it on his shoulders and goes home" (Luke 15:5-6).

Being a teenager can be rough. When we are adolescents, we are not old enough to live on our own yet but we are developed enough to make our own decisions. We begin to rebel and go off on our own to make the big decisions we are given by ourselves. The problem with growing up on our own is that we really do need a parent's guidance.

We forget Who our ultimate Guardian is and everything He can do to help us grow with Him and in Him. He provides, He cares, and He loves like a true Father. He will leave the 99 and find us, the rogue lamb. He will joyfully lift us up, and we will go home and will grow together.

Choosing God in Our Lives
~ Lauren Moody ~

We are always taught that God chose us. He's always there for us no matter what. He died for our sins and cares about us, but sometimes we forget to remember that a relationship takes effort from both sides.

My whole life I've been Seventh-day Adventist and have been taught about God. Trying to find an outlet that will teach me about Him was not an issue for me. I always had Bible class and no matter what I did He was incorporated in my life; I didn't have to try. But as I got older, it became harder for me. I still went to church and prayed, but I wasn't doing my part. I never took enough time to reach out to Him. I started to put other things before Him, such as school, friends, or volleyball.

Volleyball has become a huge part of my life. It took up a lot of time, with practices almost every night and tournaments on the weekends. I cared about it so much that, without even realizing it, I started to block God out of my life. It wasn't that I was trying to, but I didn't make enough time for Him. I put my sport before my relationship.

I've realized that choosing to put God first is just as important as Him choosing us. We want to have a relationship with Him, but that means making sure God is a number-one priority. Choosing to let Him be involved in your life and opening up to Him is crucial.

God loves us so much that He died for us. He has given us everything, and all He wants us to do is choose Him, put Him above everything else, and love Him with all our heart.

God Heard Me
~ Rio Moore ~

"And this is the confidence that we have toward Him, that if we ask anything according to His will He hears us" (1 John 5:14).

When I was in fourth grade, I was lost in the woods. As a fourth grade girl, obviously I sobbed, and in the midst of that weeping, I cried out to God. There wasn't any feelings of Him being super close to me, but I still prayed because I had learned that God hears everyone, and that's true, or else I may not have written this devotional.

God heard my crying, my prayer, and my fears. He heard it all. If He could hear my simple "Jesus, help me. Get me out of here," then why wouldn't He be able to hear anyone else who asks for his help?

Faith
~ Christian Morris ~

"Be strong and courageous. Do not be afraid or terrified because of them, for the Lord your God goes with you; He will never leave you nor forsake you" (Deuteronomy 31:6 NIV). It's very hard to have strength in hard times, but if we believe in God and trust in Him, we can do anything. From viruses, to riots, to social distancing, the year 2020 has been quite devastating. While dealing with so much negative stuff happening, it's very easy to lose faith and trust in God, but we must be strong! This is all a part of a bigger plan that the Lord has in store.

A huge part of winning the battle against fear and negativity is to trust and have faith in God. No matter how dark it gets, as long as we have faith in the Lord, we don't have to be afraid. The story of Daniel and the lion's den portrays this faith perfectly. When Daniel was thrown into the lion's den, he was probably feeling very afraid, but he put his trust in God and prayed. As long as we put our faith and trust in the Lord, we don't ever have to be afraid.

Do unto Others
~ Alana Nash ~

"And as ye would that men should do to you, do ye also to them likewise" (Luke 6:31 KJV).

One day when I was around 10 or 11, I was in a gas station getting a pack of gum. As I went up to the counter to buy it, the man behind me said he would pay for it, and to get something else as well. I went and grabbed a bag of Sugar Babies then walked back to the counter. The nice man paid for it and left, after I said thank you of course.

This past summer I was at the beach with one of my friends. We went to the Snack Shack at the beach to get ice cream. We walked up and were about to go in when I saw a little girl there. I asked her if she was going in or not, and she said that she didn't know if it was open because she couldn't read yet. I told her that it was open, and she went in with us. We walked up to the counter, and she was going to get something, but she didn't have money. So I got her an ice cream because I remembered how happy it made me when that guy bought me the gum and Sugar Babies all those years ago. I hope that she will remember that experience and do it to someone else someday, like I did with her. I hope the little girl will remember to do unto others as you want them to do unto you, like the Bible tells you to in Luke. One small action can go a long way, so think about what you do and always do unto others.

We Are All Chosen
~ Owen Officer ~

When I was four years old, I was taken from my family and put into foster care. I went through three foster homes before I came to the Officer family where I was treated like a normal kid. I finally had brothers and sisters to play with, which was new and exciting but also a little scary for the first couple of weeks. I was a foster kid for a year at their house.

It was December 2, 2011, at 7:15 pm when I got a call. I had never been called before, so I was excited. When I answered the phone, the person on the other end of the line said that he wanted to ask me a few questions. So, I answered them. Then he said he had one more question for me. He asked if I liked staying with the Officer family and if I did whether I would like to live with them permanently. It was the happiest moment of my life; I had a family that loved me and who wanted to take care of me.

Some people say you do not get to choose your family, but in some cases you can. You also can choose to be in the family of God. I never fit in until I went to live with the Officers, but now I know God had it all planned out before I knew it. In Jeremiah 29:11, we read, *"For I know the plans I have for you declares the Lord they are plans for good and not for disaster, plans to give you a future and a hope."*

Glowstick
~ Peyton Oliver ~

"But they that wait upon the Lord shall renew their strength; they shall mount up with wings as eagles; they shall run, and not be weary; and they shall walk, and not faint" (Isaiah 40:31).

In 2004, about a year before I was born, my parents brought home a little black ball of fur. Her name was Chloe, and she was a German shepherd/Labrador retriever mix. She was there when I was born and through my toddler years. She was always around through elementary school, and I couldn't imagine life without her. Chloe was there when I left for school, and there to greet me when I came back home later that day. She got older and older until, in 2016 when she was 13 years old, she started slowing down. My parents saw it coming and told us she might not make it. Chloe died that year, and it was terrible for next few weeks adjusting to life without her.

Life has its ups and downs, and sometimes it seems like we will never get out of the holes that we get into. But think of it as a glowstick that you need to break for it to shine. Now I have two young labs, Cora and Riley, but I will always miss Chloe and the impact she had on my life.

Definitions
~ Kaelyn Olson ~

Family: I feel like there are so many definitions to such a seemingly simple word. It can be thought of as your biological family, or people that you deeply care about. I personally think of family as people I care about who also care about me. Not the kind of care where you don't want some random person to die, but the kind of care that means you would do anything for them.

Friends: People whom you can trust completely with the deepest parts of yourself. People whom you are comfortable with to be you, your actual self. My definition is like this because I have found that just because you thought that someone should be there for you like you are for them, whether they are family or friends, does not mean they will be.

In Proverbs 27:17 it says, *"As iron sharpens iron, so one person sharpens another."* In my mind I feel like this means that if you associate yourself with people that make you better and you make them better, you will be happy. This principle is also there if you maintain a loving relationship with God. Your friends or family might not be there all the time, but God always will be.

Lost and Found
~ Abby Pagotelis ~

Have you ever felt lost, either spiritually or physically? I can specifically remember one time I got lost when I was five years old. My family and I went to this huge store called Cabela's. I was so mesmerized by fish in a giant tank that I didn't notice my parents had walked away without me. I turned around expecting them to be standing there, but they were gone. A lot of thoughts swarmed through my head, *"Did they forget about me?" "Will they leave without me?" "Am I ever going to find them?"* I ran around the store frantically trying to find them, but despite my efforts I could not. I wanted to ask someone for help, but I made up my mind that I could find them on my own. I searched for what seemed like hours trying to find them when over the intercom I heard my name being called to the front. I ran all the way to the front to find my eager parents waiting with their arms open.

This story reminds me that God is always searching for us no matter what. Sometimes we need to trust Him that everything will be okay. Going through life thinking you can do everything on your own and don't need God's help can be dangerous. If I would've stayed where my parents left me, they would have come back to find me. However, because I thought I had it under control and did not trust that they would come back for me, I got lost. Joshua 1:5 says, *"I will be with you. I will not leave you or forsake you."* God will never stop searching for us. All we need to do is trust that He will always come looking for us when we are lost.

The Broken Picture
~ Kale Patzer ~

God has always been here and will always be here. Many people believe He is just some guy floating around and watching us while we do things, but that is not true. God is a Father that you can turn to when everything goes wrong. He is the one you can go to when you're excited or joyful, and He is the one that will help you every single time.

When I was about six years old, my dad had a picture on his dresser of him, his dad, and me as a baby. I loved this picture and would look at it most days I walked by his room.

One day I decided that I wanted a closer look, but it was on a dresser that towered over me. This was not going to be a problem for me, though, because I knew where we kept a little stool for me to reach higher. I was able to get it down with no problem and admired it for a while until it no longer interested me. I went to put it back up when the inevitable happened. It slipped out of my hands.

As it was slowly falling, I thought of how I would have to explain to my dad what happened. I was very ashamed of myself for doing this because my dad loved that picture. After a while of having guilt built up, I decided to tell my dad about what happened. I was expecting him to be very mad at me, but he forgave me for what I did.

God is very much the same way. Once we bring our wrong to Him, He will take the sin, and forgive us forever.

"If we confess our sins, He is faithful and just to forgive us our sins and to cleanse us from all unrighteousness" (1 John 1:9).

How God Changed My Life
~ Kyrie Patzer ~

When I was very young and immature, I would do super obnoxious things to get attention. One time my teacher asked if I had any brothers or sisters. I said no.

He asked, "What about Kale?"

"He's just an animal," I replied.

Other times at school I would hide people's binders and pull out their chairs as they sat down. At the time I thought it was funny and people would laugh. Now it feels really stupid. It makes me realize as I get older that my value is not in popularity or seeking attention. It's in who God says I am.

Psalm 139:4 says, *"I praise you because I am fearfully and wonderfully made; Your works are wonderful, I know that full well."*

Sometimes it's hard to remember that when we look at our imperfections. I'm glad that God has always watched out for me. I can trust Him.

Coming Joy
~ Hannah Perine ~

I felt everything so strongly. It all became too much, and eventually it all just turned off like a light switch. In seventh grade I remember two weeks before Christmas break, I would catch myself staring at other girls; they were so thin compared to me. They were pretty and had flat stomachs with straight blonde hair. I always skipped breakfast and lunch. For dinner I would make my portions close to nothing. I became excessive with this routine and started counting my calories. I would weigh myself twice a day. I was in control, or at least I felt like it. The look or even smell of food would make me sick. My fingers and hands would be so cold they would turn a light blue, and I would get dizzy if I walked or stood up too quickly. I was labeled anorexic and bulimic by my doctors. This is when I knew I had a problem.

Being here at UCA has opened my eyes to many things, I do not feel alone anymore, but instead I feel safe and welcome by the staff and students. I remember the day of registration when I first walked into my empty dorm room I felt like a boulder had been lifted off my shoulders and I felt happy. Going through this struggle made me realize I can help other people who may be going through the same thing, or at the very least be there for them and comfort them. *"I loved you at your darkest,"* Romans 5:8 states. Romans 8:18 also states, *"The pain you've been feeling can not compare to the joy that is coming."* These two quotes from the Bible help comfort me throughout my journey and remind me that God loves me and has a plan for me.

Finding Peace
~ Linden Peterson ~

Do you ever have so much on your mind that you lie awake thinking all night? During the first two weeks of school, I felt like had no break from the constant mental strain. It seemed like every night I would lie awake thinking about homework and sports. Every morning I woke-up feeling horrible. As I got ready for the day, I stressed about my unfinished homework. Instead of focusing in class, I just thought about what I needed to do in my next class.

During all the time I spent thinking and stressing, building my relationship with God was always something I said I would work on later. At the end of the second week, I was so stressed that I needed to find some way to give my mind a break. For some reason I decided to drop everything I was thinking about and go read the Bible. As I read, everything on my mind washed away, and I felt peace. Now, I know how good our Lord is, and the only way to find peace is through Him. *"Peace I leave with you, My peace I give to you; not as the world gives do I give to you. Let not your heart be troubled, neither let it be afraid"* (John 14:27).

Chosen Children
~ Anna Phillips ~

"I will be a Father to you, and you will be my sons and daughters, says the Lord Almighty" (2 Corinthians 6:18).

Growing up, you might have once thought you were alone, or that you were just a lowly, unimportant person, and you might still feel that. But when you pray or fall back to the Bible, you find you can't be any of these things. God will not leave you alone; He will not give up on you, because He chose you.

When I was younger, my dad was building us a playhouse and my brother and I were following him around. I climbed up to the unfinished tube, which was just a platform above the ground at this time, and sat on the ledge, eight feet above the ground. I had long, heavy hair and when I flipped it out of the way, I flipped my whole body off the side. My father was working beside me on the platform and suddenly thrust his hand out to catch me by my ankle. I dangled from his hand by my one ankle and looked at my dad, wide eyed, before bursting out crying.

I was kept safe that day by my guardian angel and my Father in heaven, God. I could have gotten seriously injured if they hadn't been watching over me. All of you are being watched by God too, God has a plan that He needs you for, and He'll keep you safe and help you through the hard times because He loves you. Just when we throw ourselves off the ledge and into darkness, God is there to catch us by the ankles. God chose us to be children of God. He will be our Father, and we will be His sons and daughters.

Faith in God
~ Angela Pielaet ~

Have you ever felt like God was ignoring you? Or, have you felt that God was not hearing you?

Matthew in the Bible says, *"Jesus answered and said unto them, verily I say unto you, if ye have faith and doubt not, ye shall not only do this which is done to the fig tree, but also if ye shall say unto this mountain, Be thou removed, and be thou cast into the sea: it shall be done"* (Matthew 21:21, NKJ).

I like this verse because it tells me that when I communicate to God, I know that God hears me. God intimately knows us so well that He even knows what we think before we ask. Even though it may not be the answer that we want to hear, God loves us so much that He will always provide an answer that is the best for our well-being.

Having faith is such an important state of mind in life. Faith is knowing that God is real, cares, and loves us most of all, without being able to physically interact with Him. Faith is the foundation to having a relationship with God. God naturally reaches out to us every day and provides us with the love we need to survive, and in-turn allows us to love Him back. We must decide each day to open our hearts and allow Him access into our lives through daily communication.

Moments
~ Mia Pierce ~

Our lives are made up of moments. Our memories are filled with the moments that made us happy and the moments that made us sad. We remember the moments when we were in pain and the moments that we were at peace. Life is just one moment after the next, a never-ending cycle of emotions. Sometimes, all these little moments start to build up. Maybe you failed a test, slept through your alarm and were late for work, or maybe you are just having a bad day. All the moments that could be remembered are clumped into one massive ball of unhappiness.

These are the times when we must look around us. God knows every moment of our lives. He has it all planned out down to the second. He knows exactly when these bad moments start to become too much. That is when He sends us something good. If we slow down, open our eyes, and look around, we start to see the happy little moments God sends us.

So, what does all this even mean? It means that we always need to be on the lookout and take advantage of the opportunities God gives us. Look for the joyful moments, even when our life seems to be filled with gloomy ones. God knows exactly what we need. All we have to do is trust Him and remember that He has filled our lives with happy moments. Sometimes we just need to look a little harder to find them.

Restore Your Treasures in Heaven
~ Tearsa Pooler ~

We tend to put objects and people above God. To put God first, we need to be able to put all our trust in Him, so He can take over the things we used to think were more important. Exodus 20:3 says, *"You shall have no other Gods before Me."* Sometimes we think so highly about our friends or things that we put them above God. If we just focus on putting God first, He will do everything else for us.

I know that I put people above God. I need to work on trusting Him more because He will do so much more for me once I put Him first. Not only will He give me eternal life later, but I also will be able to see Him working in my life right now. John 10:10 says, *"I came that they may have life and have it abundantly."* God will give us an abundant life once we put Him first.

Miracle
~ Adam Powell ~

When I was six my mom got my 13-year old brother Daniel and me a trampoline. It was a black trampoline that seemed huge at the time, probably due to me being so little. One day Daniel jumped super close to get me to go super high. He jumped me so high that I couldn't land correctly. When I landed, my foot went sideways and it felt like my leg broke. I started crying as all the pain flowed in like a flash flood. At the emergency room the doctor thought it was surely broken by the way it swelled black and blue so quickly. They took x-rays, but could not tell if my leg was broken because of the swelling. They gave me crutches and an air brace until they could cast it.

The next day my mom said, "Let's pray over your leg because God can heal you!" After prayer she took me to school. At recess I wanted to go play, but the teacher would not let me go off the pavement due to my crutches in fear I might fall. I remembered our prayer. I put my crutches down and started walking without pain. My teacher asked why I was not using my crutches, and I told her my leg was fine. We had prayed over it this morning, and God healed it. Mom picked me up from school that day baffled at me not having crutches. She took me to the doctor to have another set of x-rays done, and it was not broken.

"Therefore I tell you, whatever you ask in prayer, believe that you have received it, and it will be yours" (Mark 11:24).

"O Lord my God, I cried to you for help, and You have healed me" (Psalm 30:2).

Give Him Your Burdens
~ Zoe Ramos ~

We have all been scared, stressed, and worried. It's become human nature to worry about things, and sometimes, we even end up letting them take over our lives. We tend to focus on the little things and the bad things that happen and forget the good memories. When my parents ask me if I remember anything from when I was a baby, one of the only things I remember was when we went to this beach and my parents were going to go scuba diving. I was too scared to do it since I was only around two or three years old, so my parents left me on the boat. I cried and got so scared because I thought they would leave me there and wouldn't come back for me. I can still vividly remember that experience.

There are some horrible things that happen in this world like death, wars, and sicknesses, but I believe that through all of it, we should also look at the blessings that God has given us. We have to set aside all our burdens and let Him take care of them. God promised to end all our suffering and pain as long as we let Him. He gave His only Son to die on the cross for us to prove that. It may be hard, especially in the conditions we live in at this moment, but try to look at the bright side of things and remember that it's only a matter of time until God comes and takes us to Heaven.

"Don't worry about anything; instead, pray about everything. Tell God what you need . . . Then you will experience God's peace . . . His peace will guard your hearts and minds as you live in Christ Jesus" (Philippians 4:6-7 NLT).

Fear Not
~ Amy Ranette ~

"Fear not, for I am with you; be not dismayed for I am your God" (Isaiah 41:10).

Fear. A word that holds so much meaning, something that happens to all of us. Several months ago I found myself in a scary situation. Two of my brothers and I decided to hike to an abandoned cabin about a mile from our house. Thing was, it was getting dark. I had a flashlight in my pocket, and my dog Skye on a leash. As we reached the cabin, my older brother went to check out some old cars behind the house, and my younger brother went with him. I decided to stay in front of the cabin and wait with Skye. A few minutes slowly passed, and it began to grow darker and darker. By now I was a little uneasy. I tried calling out for my brothers, but they didn't answer. By now it was even darker, and the front of the house loomed up like a dark wall.

Then I did something dumb. I took off. I started charging through the dark, down a hill with lots of brush. As I reached the bottom, I realized I was lost. I asked God to help me find the road in the dark so I could get home. After a few minutes of walking, I finally found the spot where we had left our bikes and was able to ride my bike the rest of the way home. The point is, fear can be unavoidable and sometimes uncontrollable. Have you ever felt really afraid? I'm sure we all have at one point. The next time you feel afraid, pray about it. Ask God to take your fear away and to be with you.

Walking with God
~ Claira Rees-Robins ~

"As ye have therefore received Christ Jesus the LORD, so walk ye in him" (Colossians 2:6).

I always have questioned how people walk with the LORD. I never understood it. It's hard to read the Bible all the time, especially when you can be playing on your phone or watching TV. Also, what about that still small voice people always talk about, or the shout they hear from nowhere warning them not to do something? That's never happened to me. But that's not what counts. God doesn't talk to or get all people's attention in the same way.

This might seem silly, but maybe God is calling you in a different way. It doesn't have to be something big. I always wonder why I haven't had a huge experience that has changed my life. But all the little things you do, all the small changes you make in your lifestyle that bring you closer to God are what counts. Even if you don't feel like reading your Bible, praying, and being kind, just do it. The small things count. When you receive Jesus, just walk in the way that best fits you, and that will draw you close to God.

The Faith of a Boy
~ Adrian Reeves ~

Did you know that even the smallest of brothers can have more faith than a giant? Well its true! There was once a giant whose name was Goliath and most everyone in Israel feared him, at nine feet tall with armor weighing over a hundred pounds! Saul's army cowered in fear when they saw his height and heard his booming voice, but there was one boy that wasn't afraid, nor trained for battle, he was faithful to God and understood that God could do anything.

"David said to the Philistine 'You come against me with sword and spear and javelin, but I come against you in the name of the Lord Almighty, the God of the armies of Israel whom you have defied'... So David triumphed over the Philistine with a sling and a stone; without a sword in his hand he struck down the Philistine and killed him" (1 Samuel 17:45 and 50, NIV).

Now you've probably read the story of David and Goliath, but did you also know that we face our own giants? I believe they are referred to as mountains in the Bible, for Jesus said: *"Because you have so little faith. Truly I tell you, if you have faith as small as a mustard seed, you can say to this mountain 'move from here to there,' and it shall move. Nothing shall be impossible for you"* (Matthew 17:20 NIV). Now, I don't believe that a mountain can move in location, but rather that He was speaking of mountains blocking our paths to Him, such as fear, or temptation, or even jealousy. I think He was speaking in a parable like He did so many times in the New Testament.

I hope this gives you a different view to better understand God.

Choose Wisely
~ Kailey Reitz ~

We have all heard it hundreds of times before, "You can't choose your family, but you can choose your friends." However, most people do not stop to think about what that means. You can create a community of people that comes together based purely on common interests or hobbies. Personalities, interests, and morals of those you spend the most time with will eventually rub off on you because these people can become your adopted family. It can be a wonderful thing, or it can be a bad thing if the people you spend time with are not the best influences. You can probably point out the bullies in your life and say that you will never act like that or do those things. Yet when you hang out with the wrong people, they can turn from kind people into bullies very quickly. Good friends rub off on you in a positive way, through the experiences you go through and the conversations you have. You could have the best times of your life if you are with the right people. Be careful with the people you choose to have as your friends because they can turn into your family.

"Jesus told Simon, 'Don't be afraid! From now on you will bring in people instead of fish.' The men pulled their boats up on the shore. Then they left everything and went with Jesus" (Luke 5:10-11). Just like Jesus chose His disciples wisely, we need to choose our friends wisely. Friends are there to support you, to love you, and to make memories with you. Don't forget to choose wisely.

God is our Guide
~ Spencer Rich ~

One year ago, during my last years at a small elementary school, our eighth grade class and staff prepared for our annual eighth grade rafting trip. For many, this experience of being washed down a swirling river with a team of friends was completely new and a bit intimidating. Nevertheless, the whole of our class was enthusiastic and excited to start this adventure. Early one morning, we loaded our transport busses to the brim with sleeping bags and luggage for the overnight stay at our campgrounds. While the prospect of a long bus ride was dreaded by my classmates, the edge of our anticipation kept us happily waiting to arrive. Once we unpacked and settled our belongings, we went white-water rafting for the very first time.

Our rafts, packed full of energetic students and a guide who was trained to know the uncertain waters, set off. Through the calm passages and the violent lurches of that wild river, our guide gave instruction and guidance to us, all the while using his paddle to steer our raft towards the safest path. It was calming to me to know that we were not alone in this unfamiliar place, that the one guiding us knew what he was doing. In the same way, God guides our lives through any unpredictable waters or struggles in our life—especially when we trust in Him and ask for His guidance. Jeremiah 29:11 says, *"'For I know the plans I have for you,' declares the Lord, 'plans to prosper you and not to harm you, plans to give you hope and a future.'"* No matter if you see it in your daily life or not, God has a plan for us—better than any plan we could make.

God's Plan
~ Jason Roberts ~

I was only in second grade when my grandfather was killed. The crash site was viewable from my house. All my emotions in the next three days were all up in the air until the funeral. I remember the day the crash happened. I was picked up from school, told that my grandpa was killed, taken to the larger airport to pick up my dad, and then driven to the scene. By the time we had surveyed the scene and visited my grandmother, I had had enough of all the people, emotions, and confusion. So, quietly, I spaced out with my friends. And to this day, the best thing about that whole situation was time spent with friends.

This was not the only situation like this. I have had others quite similar to this. But every time, my friends have been there for me. Always remember that God is there for you, and that everything that happens in this world happens for a purpose. God has not forgotten you, God has not stopped loving you, and God is not punishing you. God is your friend when things just are not going right; He is always there for you. God will never give up on you, and He will never leave, so why should you leave Him? This is just one example of how God has shaped me into the person I am today. God shapes everybody in different ways.

"See I have refined you, though not as silver; I have tested you in the furnace of affliction" (Isaiah 48:10).

The Crash
~ Tommy Rogers ~

One afternoon I was out riding dirt bikes with a few of my friends. This was a new place where I had never ridden, and I was not familiar with the trail. We were riding on a small skinny path only one or two feet wide, and on the right side of the path was the side of a mountain, and to the left was the very steep side of the mountain going down. I had ridden on trails like this before, but the trail was still all new to me and I had to keep my eye on it the whole time to avoid rocks and roots jutting out into the path. I also was riding a new bike for the first time and was very excited because it was bigger and better than my last bike. As time went on, I got more and more comfortable and felt like I was in total control, and I started to go faster.

Eventually, I got so comfortable that I had slowly stopped paying attention to the path, and out of nowhere a rock popped up in front of me and sent me off the path and down the side of the mountain. As I slid down, I felt I was never going to stop, but I did, 20 feet down from the trail. It took us almost an hour to pull my bike back up.

If I had kept my eyes on the path, I wouldn't have fallen. We need to keep our eyes on God so that we can avoid obstacles in our way and stay on the path.

He is There
~ Ethan Sanchez ~

Like most of you, I was raised going to church every Sabbath for my whole life. I was homeschooled up to sixth grade, and after that I went to a tiny school were my eigth grade class was five people, including me. Going to church ended up being more for me to see my friends than going to learn about God. If I'm honest, it's still like that most of the time. I don't really have a close relationship with God.

Two years ago, my mom died of cancer. I am not saying that's the reason I'm not close to God, but it didn't help. Every day I prayed for her to get better and every day she got worse. What I am trying to say is that bad things happen in our lives that we don't understand, and those can affect our relationship with God. But although I didn't see Him then in my own life, I've seen Him in my family's. Look around and see what God is doing. Just because you cannot see Him in your life doesn't mean He's not there.

Keep Going
~ Danerose Sanford ~

"'For I know the plans I have for you,' declares the LORD, 'plans to prosper you and not to harm you, plans to give you hope and a future'" (Jeremiah 29:11).

Do you have a goal or a dream that you want to chase? Well, what are you waiting for? Go chase your fantasy. Even though your friends or family might not approve of it, you should just go for it. Do what you love; be confident in what you want to do in life. You don't need other people to tell you what you need or what you have to do.

This year I just started high school and a few people asked me, "What do you want to be when you're older?" That question had me thinking for a little bit. Everyone knows that I like music, and that I am very musically talented. I also like detective work. When I was younger, I would secretly spy on my parents and hide things around the house. Sometimes my parents wouldn't find it until a few weeks later because I hid it so well. Other than detective work, I also like a few other things. So, I don't yet know how to answer their question. I just know that whatever happens I will be happy with it because I know God chose that specific job for me. Never give up on your dreams. If you fail, keep on trying until you make it. You will never know what God has in store for you, me, and well basically everyone. Just keep going.

There Is Hope!
~ Hailey Schmid ~

Have you ever felt alone? Or like you don't matter? Many times in my life I have felt this way. It's hard to think that you're not important to anyone; it's something that always brings tears to my eyes. It's been a constant battle, wondering if I matter, if I'm good enough, or if I belong in this world. I struggle with not loving myself because I'm adopted. At times it's such a struggle that I feel depressed, alone, and like no one will understand what I'm going through. For the longest time I felt rejected and hurt by my birthparents, and I reflected others off my birthparents. I saw the world through dark colored lenses and trusted no one. I put walls up so no one could hurt me again. I went to a therapeutic boarding school and worked hard and changed so much into a new and awesome person!

Yes, I still struggle. Yes, things still hurt me at times. But I'm not the same person that I once was; I'm the best me that I can be now. In 2 Corinthians 5:17 it says, *"Therefore if anyone is in Christ he is a new creation, the old has gone, the new has come."* Believe in yourself, believe that you are enough, believe that you do matter, believe that when you fall you can get back up, dust yourself off, and not give up because you are important.

I leave you with one thing: God knows that you are good enough, you just have to trust Him and believe it yourself. God has a plan for you. God protected me and gave me an awesome family who loves me. So love yourself, believe that you can do it, and believe that you are chosen.

Digging Deeper
~ Makenna Shiranzadeh ~

When I was eleven, my family and I went snow skiing at a resort called Silver Mountain. It had snowed 31 inches the night before we went so there was powder everywhere. We decided to go on one of our favorite runs called North Face Glades. There were about five other people who had gone on that run before we had, so the snow was very untracked. After every turn, huge piles of fluffy snow would follow me. I was having so much fun trying to out-ski the snow that I wasn't paying much attention to where I was going.

All of the sudden, my skis crossed and I soon realized I wasn't skiing anymore. I had fallen in a tree well and the snow from the tree had fallen on top of me so I couldn't see where I was. I tried to get up, but I couldn't move! The snow was starting to pack around me because I kept wiggling. I was starting to freak out because my family was ahead of me and they didn't see me fall.

I soon realized that if I was going to get out of there, I should start praying. I asked God to send someone to help get me out of there. Right then, I heard my dad's voice. He told me to stop moving because I was only digging myself deeper. As he was helping dig me out, I realized that just like my dad, God will always be there to help dig us out of trouble, and He will always be there no matter what.

Joshua 1:9 says, *"Be strong and courageous; do not be frightened or dismayed, for the Lord you God is there with you wherever you go."*

My Own Red-Billed Oxpecker
~ Haylee B. Simpson ~

"I will say of the Lord, 'He is my refuge and my fortress, my God, whom I trust'" (Psalms 92:2).

The Red-billed Oxpecker is a passerine bird that is native to the savannah of sub-Saharan Africa. This beautiful bird has a bright red beak, along with orange and red circling its eyes. This makes the bird almost look like it's a warning, and it's not just looks that make this bird give off such presence. The oxpecker sits on the back of mammals and not only eats the bugs right off them, but also alerts the unsuspecting animal it's sitting on to nearby danger with a sharp call.

This specifically helps rhinos, who are alerted immediately after the bird spots human poachers. Studies have shown that without the Red-Billed Oxpecker, rhino's were only able to sense danger of nearby humans 23 percent of the time. But with the oxpecker, they sensed the humans every single time. The relationship between the two animals is one full of much-needed trust, and without it, the rhino would be in lots of danger and incredibly lost.

I like to think of God as my Red-billed Oxpecker. Not only does He help with the little things like how the bird helps with the mammals' ticks, but He also helps steer me away from danger every time without fail. Of course for this relationship to work, trust is needed, and without that foundation, I would certainly be lost. On my own, I can't see the temptations and dangers surrounding me. But with God, I will gladly be warned and protected from any nearby danger as long as I place my trust in Him.

Rollercoaster Fears
~ Kailianne Smart ~

"I can do all things through Christ who strengthens me."
(Philippians 4:13)

I have always been terrified of rollercoasters because they would always make me feel sick. But last year for my eigth grade gift, a couple of my friends decided to take me to Disneyworld! Well, in all that excitement and awesomeness, there was one part that was not so awesome to me. A lot of what we were going to do was ride on rollercoasters. Now, when my parents found this out, they decided that I needed to go on the worst rollercoaster we had around! I did not want to do it, but did I have a choice? No. So, the day had come, and I had to ride a rollercoaster called "The Monster." It is a huge rollercoaster that is super-fast, dumps you upside down a bunch of times, takes you straight up, and dangles you just by your legs (because that's all of you it is holding onto). It was not an easy fear for me to get over, but by the end of that day I went home as a person who loved rollercoasters, and I couldn't wait to get to Disneyworld to ride all the other rollercoasters they had.

God can help you get over any fears you have, from a fear of rollercoasters to public speaking. There is no fear in the world that God cannot help you overcome; all you have to do is ask Him. When you give your fears to God, He can help you get over them and make your life more fun in the meantime, *"For I can do all things through Christ who strengthens me."*

Fun Times
~ Bella Smith ~

"The temptations in your life are no different from what others experience. And God is faithful. He will not allow the temptation to be more than you can stand. When you are tempted, he will show you a way out so that you can endure" (1 Corinthians 10:13).

The sun was shining bright up at Schweitzer Mountain. The powder was thick and soft from the previous night's snowfall. My friends and I decided that it would be a great idea to go into some untouched powder. We ducked the rope like the bad kids that we are. We went into a valley of snow which had a creek at the bottom. We went all the way down to the bottom of the creek. Within a few seconds we had put ourselves into deep trouble, but we didn't realize it yet. We took off our skis and immediately sank waist-deep into the fluffy powder. That is when we realized that we were in deep trouble. My friend and my sister started making a trail by packing down the snow. I called another friend that was skiing to come help us. After I called the friend, I started chucking the skis up the hill one by one. After doing this for an hour and a half we were more than halfway there. My friend that was with us, sunk down and got his foot caught in a root. We spent 30 minutes with our gloves deep in the snow, working his foot out from under the root. We finally got him out, and then we kept hiking out for another 45 minutes. Finally, I let out a sigh of relief—I could see skiers! We got out after two hours of hiking. This shows that you can get into sin in four seconds, but it can take hours to get out of it. It was a great life lesson learned.

My Grandfather's Passing
~ Chase Smith ~

My father's family has always had a close relationship. We still endure plenty of drama, but that's just family. Over the summer, the head of the family, my grandfather, passed. A few years back he was diagnosed with Parkinson's disease, and each year he had been growing weaker. Sadly, this year the Parkinson's caught up.

During his last week, the whole family gathered to spend time with him and say goodbye. While we were there, we would play games and laugh and enjoy time together. But every night when we went to check on him, the mood in the room became very serious. I started to think how if it were not for him, none of us would have been there (except my grandma). The whole time a radio played some quiet Sabbath music.

The last few nights we would do short Bible studies. My oldest cousin, Hannah, would read a story from the Bible and we would all just sit and listen. We were not sure if my grandfather was even aware of what was happening around him, but we hoped he was enjoying everyone's presence. One night we were trying to decide whether to read or leave him to get some rest. So, my aunt asked him, and he simply responded, "Read."

Three nights later my grandfather passed away late at night. He cared a lot about his family and his connection to God. Whenever I think about my relationship with God, I think about him and his faith as a gold standard. He was a great man and is missed greatly by all his family and friends.

"We love each other because He loved us first" (1 John 4:19).

Am I chosen?
~ Ethan Smith ~

My childhood was not the best, but it was not the worst. My mother was a drug addict most of my life and as a result, she was not there and I never got the attention I needed. My biological father left when I was two years old and the other two men she married were physically and verbally abusive. My uncle sexually abused me when I was seven. All these things made me mature faster than I should have and made me realize things about life that kids should not even be thinking about. Even though all this happened, can God still choose me to do good for Him?

I believe, even though I had to experience things, God still has a purpose for me. The problem can arise when you tell yourself that you are useless and cannot do anything for God. If you let God work in your life, not only will He work in it, but He will bless it and find a way for you to do good for Him. I am still a work in progress and sometimes I doubt whether or not I am useful to God, but I do know that once I let God into my life, I realized there were good things I could find out of the bad. I realized I could relate, sympathize, and empathize with people. I could use my ability to do this to show people the character of God. So, if you ever doubt that God can choose you, remember that God already chose you for something amazing!

Having Courage
~ Alissa Stafford ~

I don't like playing the guitar up front typically, but my family finally convinced me to. It was a sunny and beautiful Saturday afternoon when our family led song service for church (outside due to COVID-19). I pulled out my guitar and I was ready, yet my hands were shaking and sweating so much that it was hard for me to play. I hid behind my older brother so people wouldn't see my shaking hands. After we finished, I was quite relieved and settled in to listen to the sermon. When church ended, I realized that it was going to be a while before I would be able to play with my older brother again as he would soon be heading off to college. The more I thought of this, I found myself thinking about what Peter said, *"Cast all your anxiety on Him because He cares for you"* (I Peter 5:7). Next time, instead of hiding behind my older brother, I can ask God to take my nerves and let Him be the one that people see and hear instead of me.

Chosen in More Ways Than One
~ Landyn Stam ~

Chosen. Chosen by God. Chosen by family. Chosen by friends. The list goes on and on. You can be chosen in so many ways, by so many people. When I think of being chosen, I think of adoption.

To be more specific, I think of when my family made the life-changing decision to adopt. After lots of paperwork and trips to Ethiopia and back, we finally brought Jobe Habulu Stam home. When I look back now, I can't remember my life without Jobe in it. I don't think of or refer to him as my "adopted brother" but just my sweet, silly, crazy, loving, overly-caring little brother. He fits right into the family and brings the most enormous amount of love and laughter into our lives. So even though we might not have the same blood running through our veins, we will always have the same love running through our hearts.

In the same way I could never imagine my life without Jobe in it, God can't imagine heaven without all of us in it. So just like all those years ago, God chooses each and every one of us every single day.

Saved by a Stranger
~ Kevin Stathem ~

My favorite verse that speaks to me is Psalm 119:105: *"Your word is a lamp to guide my feet, and a light for my path."* God guided me during my hardest times in my life, and He continues to help me even now! Whenever my life goes downhill, I can trust that He will guide me to Him. When I was three or four, my sister Sarah nearly fell off a cliff. My terrified yet relieved brother came rushing down to tell my mom and me what happened. He said, "Some man came up and caught Sarah, but when we looked for him to thank him, he was nowhere! We looked all over for him, and I think it was an angel!" My family thanked God for the rest of that day. As soon as we got to Sarah, we called an ambulance, and my sister got stiches on her whole bottom lip. I still think about how God saved my sister from dying, and I thank Him for the littlest blessings He gives me!

The Time I Was Chosen
~ Maxwell Stone ~

I love basketball. I have been playing basketball since I was in the fourth grade. When I picked up a basketball in fourth grade and started playing, I wasn't good. Even though I wasn't good, it was still a fun sport to play, and I knew I wanted to get better. So, I started playing as much as I could during recess. When I was in the fifth grade, I was able to try out for the basketball team at the school was attending. I was a little nervous, but I made the team.

When the season started, I didn't get much playing time in the games because I wasn't the best. Throughout my middle school years, I kept practicing basketball as much as I could, and by seventh grade, I was on the starting five for the team. But then I graduated and had to go to high school. I was very nervous about trying out for the high-school basketball team because I felt intimidated by all the upper classmen. When the tryouts came, I tried as hard as I could and was able to make the first cut, but they held another tryout for who made the team.

After the second tryout, I felt like I did horribly and that I had no chance to make the varsity team. But two weeks later, on a Sunday night before I went to bed, my sister got a text saying that I made the team! I was so excited once I heard the news that I was chosen, and I could not wait to go play on the team.

When you are nervous or depressed and are feeling like you won't be chosen, remember God has chosen you already, and you don't have to get through tryouts.

Downhill
~ Paige Sumner ~

When I was little, my best friend decided that she would teach me how to ride a bike. As the wise and elderly one-year-older person she was, I placed complete trust in her teaching methods. However, as I followed her over to where the bike sat, I started to feel uneasy, yet I decided to follow her lead. She ran inside to get me a helmet and told me to wait for her. When she did come back, and my helmet was secured to my head, she looked at me with an expression of excitement and said, "Are you ready?"

I can tell you that I most certainly was not ready for what was to come. I had imagined her slowly pushing me on the bike. However, instead she put both hands on my back and pushed as hard as she could, sending me plummeting down the hill. I would like to mention that this bike had no pedals, not to mention brakes. So, I could do nothing but let the bike take me to my unforeseen destination.

Looking back at this adventure, I have realized that it brings up an important point. While I might not have been one hundred percent trusting of my friend's idea, I still followed her and got on that bike. I showed that I had trust in her. Sometimes we are asked to trust God, and sometimes we really do not want to. However, the Bible says that the faith of a mustard seed can move a mountain. God does not ask us to immediately have unfailing trust in Him. Instead, He asks for just enough trust to give Him a try. Just like with my bike adventure, we might crash. However, with God we will always get back up and reap the benefits of putting our trust in Him just as I did indeed learn how to ride a bike with my best friend's unethical help.

When Jesus Calmed the Storm
~ Veronika Suprun ~

"Then He got into the boat and His disciples followed Him. Suddenly a furious storm came up on the lake, so that the waves swept over the boat. But Jesus was sleeping. The disciples went and woke Him, saying, 'Lord, save us! We're going to drown!'

"He replied, 'You of little faith, why are you so afraid?' Then He got up and rebuked the winds and the waves, and it was completely calm.

"The men were amazed and asked, 'What kind of man is this? Even the winds and the waves obey Him!'" (Matthew 8:23-27).

This story reminds me of what happened to my sister. She was only eight months old when she had to go to the emergency room. Everyone in my family was afraid that she might not make it. For me, I was just losing hope and faith. My family kept praying and praying while I was just sitting thinking of all the negatives of what could happen. I had a dream where a beautiful white angel came down to talk to me.

He said, "Don't be afraid, my Child, God is here."
"Clearly not!" I yelled at him. "My sister is dying!"
He placed his hand on my hand, saying, "Do you trust and believe God?"
"Yes, I do."
"Then trust in Him, Don't lose faith."

I woke up and started to begin praying and reading the Bible with my family, hoping my sister make it. After two days we got some good news--my sister would make it. It was a miracle. I've realized now that trusting in Him, even through the hardships, can produce faith.

Masterpieces
~ Missy Surdal ~

"For you formed my inward parts; you knitted me together in my mother's womb. I praise you, for I am fearfully and wonderfully made. Wonderful are your works; my soul knows it very well" (Psalms 139:13-14).

You were specifically created for a reason. Before you were even born, God knew what your personality would be like, how much you would laugh or cry, and who He could put in your life to help you through it. He took, or is ready to take, any past experiences and use them to help you grow and show His love to others.

The environment that you were raised in has continued to affect you in one way or another. Perhaps you had a family where you were one of many and constantly overlooked. Maybe you were in a situation where you had to grow up faster than most of us. Perhaps you consider your childhood pretty uneventful. Whatever your situation, these things have shaped you and made you who you are for a reason.

However, this is not implying that God made bad things happen to you. On the contrary, this shows that He takes what is broken and damaged by our sinful world and makes it a beautiful masterpiece. He has helped you throughout your whole life in ways that you cannot even imagine.

You were not an accident, especially not to God. He chose you and made you. Every part of you was made for a specific purpose. You are priceless and worth the world. God loves to take you, mold you, help you, and create a masterpiece out of you.

Unwanted
~ Madison Threadgill ~

I've always heard of people saying to get rid of the toxic people in your life, and how it's okay to get rid of friends that are mean. That is so true. I grew up in a smaller school where there weren't many people, so I had the same friends my whole life. I didn't really feel like I needed anyone else because I thought everything was fine. But I realized it's so much better when you have good friends that really care about you, friends that chose you. They aren't just stuck with you because you go to the same school. Find those friends that will hang out with you because they want to as well.

At my old school, my last year there was really hard on me. And just as it was hitting the worst part ever, where I was basically crying myself to sleep every night, the big virus happened. At first, I was sad but then very thankful. I finally was away from people that made my life harder, away from people that would make me feel bad about being myself. Thank goodness for quarantine. But then again, I had no one to talk to. That whole year I felt alone, left out, like no one wanted me. I did not feel chosen. I didn't even really feel like God wanted me at this point because none of my friends even did. I didn't talk to anyone about this for almost a whole year. It was also hard to come to God about my problems. Even when I did come to Him, I wondered if He would even listen. But He does. He helps even if we think He doesn't. Even when none of your friends chose you, God will.

Chosen to be Included
~ Gabrielle Townsend ~

"Do not let your hearts be troubled. You believe in God; believe also in Me. My Father's house has many rooms; if that were not so, would I have told you that I am going there to prepare a place for you? And if I go and prepare a place for you, I will come back and take you to be with Me that you also may be where I am" (John 3:1-3).

In elementary school I considered myself to be friends with everybody in my class. We would play at recess together, and all generally got along. As time passed, and people got older, exclusive groups started to form. You can eat with some people, but that doesn't mean they will talk to you. Just because you are partners in class doesn't mean you will hang out. It can be painful to grow apart or feel left out.

The beautiful thing about God is that you are not only chosen for a life to help others, but also chosen to be included. God is always ready to talk and will always listen. When we spend time with God, we are growing closer to Him and never apart because of Him. With God's help we can become more like Him and grow closer to the people around us who are learning to love God too. In the end, God cannot wait to have us over to His home in heaven where we will be included in the best party forever!

Prayer Life
~ Connor Turner ~

My prayer life is not full of prayer, but when I did pray, things happened. I never really prayed unless I wanted something. I'm trying to change that, but it's pretty hard. One of my earliest memories is when I lost my stuffed animal when I was five. We all know when you're a little kid that grew-up Adventist, God is like the biggest thing in your life, so of course I prayed. Two seconds later, I felt the urge to look under my bed, and there it was.

I don't remember any big prayers until I was in seventh grade. My English teacher was assigning a project. We had to do a report on a friend's back story. I was struggling on the inside wondering if I wanted to get baptized. I wanted to, but I didn't know if I was ready. I prayed on the Friday when the projects where due. My prayer was that someone would say the word baptize. Towards the end of the day, someone said that their partner got BAPTIZED on a blind date. I told my mom about my answer to prayer, I took studies, and got baptized that summer.

In eighth grade I prayed one more time for a big reason and that was about coming to UCA. I prayed that this one YouTuber in one of his videos says yes five times for me to come here, or no five times for me not to come. He said yes five times and no only once! I hope you can start praying more and trusting God with your life because He will point you in the right direction.

The Ribbon
~ Savannah Turner ~

When I was very young my mother would always read Robert Munsch writings to my sisters and me. There was always this one story we would beg my mom to read to us called "Ribbon to the Rescue." The story was about a flower girl with a ribbon dress on the way to a wedding. On her way there were many people who needed help, such as the groom who had no shoe laces and a family with an unwrapped gift. To help all of the people she came across on her way, she used her ribbons, and she got very muddy and dirty in the process. Once she got to the church where the wedding was being held, the pastor would not let her in because of the way she looked.

Looking back on this story now I can see how it relates to churches that are wrapped up in trying to look good instead of trying to show other people who Jesus is through their attitudes. In my life I have been incorporated in many churches and church events where people told me that I should not be wearing the clothes that I had on to church, and that I should only eat certain foods in order to get to heaven. Instead of being so wrapped up in outwardly appearances, we should focus on showing other people our beliefs through our persona of Jesus.

Prayer
~ Claire Twigg ~

Do you ever feel lonely, overwhelmed, anxious, or scared? These are emotions everyone feels at some point throughout their life. God gave us prayer so we can talk to Him about those things; it is our way of communicating with God so we can have a relationship with Him. Prayer has helped me by making me feel safer in scary situations and by comforting me. One time, I was watching my little sister in the store while my mom was buying groceries. We went to the toy section and I took my eyes off her for a split second. I turned around and she was gone! I was so worried about her. It felt like I was looking for her for ages! She still was nowhere to be found. As I was freaking out, I said a prayer in my head. I walked around the corner, and she was there! God helped me find my little sister. We need to remember to thank God for what He has done for us when we pray. God does listen and He wants to hear our prayers.

"Do not be anxious about anything, but in every situation, by prayer and petition, with thanksgiving, present your requests to God. And the peace of God, which transcends all understanding, will guard your hearts and your minds in Christ Jesus" (Philippians 4:6-7).

Bloody Wood Chips
~ Austin Uhrig ~

My sister was "it." We were playing a game like a playground version of Marco Polo. The selected person must close their eyes and try to find the others. If the person that's "it" calls "Wood Chips" while someone is on the wood chips, then they are "it." My sister went to where she heard me, which was on a ladder that was a part of the playground equipment. She started shaking the ladder to make me fall off. While she was shaking it, she hit her head on the ladder. It cut her forehead and blood started gushing from her forehead. I watched as it trickled down on to the woodchips, and even though I felt sorry for my sister, I realized that now I was safe from becoming "it."

This isn't a perfect analogy, but this reminded me of the Bible when the Israelites put the lamb's blood on their doors. In Exodus 12:13, God says, *"But the blood on your doorposts will serve as a sign, marking the houses where you are staying. When I see the blood, I will pass over you. This plague of death will not touch you when I strike the land of Egypt."* The blood was symbolic in the way that they were safe from death, just like how I was safe from becoming "it."

Jesus is Our Shepherd
~ Jason Ungureanu ~

Sheep are known to be wanderers; they easily stray from their flock and can get themselves into difficult situations such as getting lost, getting hurt, and putting themselves at a risk of getting attacked by other animals. This is why sheep are known to have a shepherd. A shepherd helps guide sheep when they wander off and leads them in the right direction. A shepherd protects his sheep, cares for his sheep, and always watches over his sheep.

In our religious life we can relate ourselves to sheep with Jesus being our Shepherd. When we tend to wander off our path we can get hurt and feel like we can't find our way back. That is why Jesus is our Shepherd because in times of need, He helps guide us to find our way back. He's always there to protect us and always cares for us.

Life can sometimes feel hard, and we can feel lost, but we have one of the greatest Shepherds. Just as David wrote in Psalm 23 1-6, *"The Lord is my Shepherd; I shall not want. He makes me to lie down in green pastures; He leads me beside the still waters. He restores my soul; He leads me in the paths of righteousness for His name's sake. Yea, though I walk through the valley of the shadow of death, I will fear no evil; For You are with me. Your rod and Your staff, they comfort me. You prepare a table before me in the presence of my enemies; You anoint my head with oil; My cup runs over. Surely goodness and mercy shall follow me All the days of my life; And I will dwell in the house of the Lord forever."*

Nail in My Foot
~ Jack Vogel ~

I was walking in the woods with my friends next to their house. I saw a board and I stomped on it as hard as I could, and then I let out a loud yelp. There was a nail in the board, and it went through my foot. I had to sit there with the nail through my foot for about 15 minutes.

My friends went to go get their dad. When they got back, I was crying. Not because it hurt, but because there was a nail in my foot. I thought it would be in there forever and thought I had to walk around my whole life with a nail in my foot.

We went back to their house, and I was crying so much. Eventually, they pulled it out somehow. Now I was crying because there was a hole in my foot, and I thought it would be there forever. I was so stupid.

Next, I went home and got a bandage on it. I just played games and slept the rest of the day. I think God helped me through that to not feel any pain. I am very glad that He helped through getting a nail in my foot.

"Do not be afraid or discouraged, for the LORD will personally go ahead of you. He will be with you; He will neither fail you nor abandon you" (Deuteronomy 31:8).

Prayers
~ Tucker Wallace ~

"If you believe, you will receive whatever you ask for in prayer" (Matthew 21:22).

How many of you believe God answers prayers? The Bible verse above promises answers to prayer if we only believe. I would like to tell you a story about just such an occasion.

When my older sister was about five years old, she and my dad were driving through Stockton, California, which is a city with a very high crime rate, so they were trying to get to the next town. They were driving in an old, beat up van that did not run very well at all. It was in the evening and it was getting darker.

When they were driving through South Stockton, the van broke down. They were stuck there for a little under an hour, and they had no idea what the problem was. My dad called a bunch of people to try to get help, but nothing was working out. They were starting to get very worried, so my sister decided to say a prayer, hoping that God would help them. And then they tried to start the car again. It struggled the first time, but my dad tried again, and the car started. It was a miracle.

My sister believed that when she prayed, the car would be fixed. The Bible promises that even faith as small as a mustard seed can move mountains. Sometimes all it takes is to believe and have faith like a child.

He Is Always Listening
~ Laura Wertz ~

About five years back, my family decided to move from our Oregon home to the Idaho panhandle. We found a piece of land we really liked, so we bought it. However, we didn't know at the time that the land was flooded, and that we couldn't build there. We had to sell that land and search for another place to live.

Meanwhile, the house we were living in had been on the market for a while, and we were having quite a bit of trouble selling it. We brought these issues to God in prayer, asking for His guidance. After months of stress, God finally brought us to our current home and found a family who would benefit from our old one.

"Do not be anxious about anything, but in everything, by prayer and petition, with thanksgiving, present your requests to God" (Philippians 4:6).

The Day I Fell Off
~ Chloe Whitmore ~

The day was a sunny one with a cool breeze blowing through the fields. I was out in the pasture riding a black mare. Just recently I had learned to be especially confident on a horse, and the day was the perfect day for the horse and me. As I came to the top of the hill, I gently asked her to trot; we swiftly went down the hill until, lo and behold, I was in the air. My foot got stuck in the stirrup, and I landed on my head. I sat up quickly and caught my breath, trying to find my glasses. Standing, I felt a sharp pain in my ankle. I wanted to just flop back on the grass, but I needed to get the horse, so I got the old mare, mounted, and headed to the barn.

My foot was checked out, and it was a bad tear. After being on crutches for a while, I had to think about the whole experience. It was kind of funny, me flying off a little horse and landing on my head, but I was a bit worried to get back on another horse, remembering how the horse acted.

This resembles our relationship with God. When something bad happens to us, we blame God or stop talking to Him. Then it takes us a while to get back on with God, but He keeps whispering to us. I did get back on the horse, but I always have that bit of pain in my ankle to remind me to hang on tighter to the saddle horn, and even tighter to God.

"Fear not, for I am with you; be not dismayed, for I am your God; I will strengthen you, I will help you, I will uphold you with my righteous right hand" (Isaiah 41:10).

God's Plan
- Elijah Wines -

It was the day before the Super Bowl: the Rams and the Patriots. I was nervous all night about what was going to happen the next day. That night I prayed that the Rams would shut Tom Brady down and take home the Lombardi Trophy. I thought that if I prayed the chances of the Rams winning the Super Bowl would be increased.

The next day I went over to my friend's house to watch the game. The Rams running back, Todd Gurley, was one of the best running backs that year, but for most of the game he was sitting on the sidelines because of an injury. All the other players on the offense were having trouble getting into the end zone. Whatever the Rams tried, the Patriots would stop it immediately. On the other hand, the Rams defense did very good, but not good enough. The game ended, and the Patriots won, 13-3, the lowest scoring Super Bowl in history.

What I learned out of all of this is that God does not always say yes just because you want something. God knows what the best plan is, and He can see the big picture.

"'For I know the plans I have for you,' declares the Lord, 'plans to prosper you and not to harm you, plans to give you hope and a future'" (Jerimiah 29:11).

The Feeling of Being Alone
~ Daniel Wright ~

Growing up as an only child I was often alone at home. I usually watched movies, read (kind of), played with toys, or gamed, my favorite activity! I often played games like Roblox and Minecraft with my friends. When I was not gaming, I watched YouTube. If my friends weren't online and I got bored of everything else, I was kind of depressed. I ate lots of food. I browsed the web (which without a lot of supervision does not seem like a good idea). But I was missing something. I felt alone and did not know what my worth was. Sure, I went to church, had Sabbath school, and I knew God, but did I really have a good relationship with Him?

At one point I got suicidal. I did not tell anyone, but I made bad jokes about me being dead and shared them with my friends who got concerned. I had stopped reading the Bible, praying, and stopped caring about God. Each day I thought about my friends and family and asked myself if they cared at all about me. Then one day I decided to flip through the Bible (only God knows how I made that decision) and I found a specific Bible verse:

"The righteous cry and the Lord hears and delivers them out of all their troubles. The Lord is near to the brokenhearted and saves those who are crushed in spirit. Many are the afflictions of the righteous, but the Lord delivers him out of them all. He keeps all his bones, not one of them is broken, evil shall slay the wicked, and those who hate the righteous will be condemned. The Lord redeems the soul of His servants, and none of those who take refuge in him will be condemned" (Psalm 34:17-20).

True Peace
~ Abby Young ~

What is peace? The dictionary defines peace as "freedom from disturbance; tranquility." But what does that mean, and where do we find peace? John 14:27 says, *"Peace I leave with you, my peace I give unto you; not as the world gives, do I give to unto you. Do not let not your heart be troubled neither let it be afraid."* That is our answer. The Bible tells us that God will give us true peace, not worldly peace. We cannot have or find peace in the world.

For the last nine years, I have been homeschooled. Coming to UCA has been a pretty big change for me. Learning how to manage my time and getting used to the schoolwork and dorm life has been quite stressful at times. Whenever I get caught up in the stressors of school, I talk to my parents and they *always* remind me to pray for peace.